Reflections from the Pond

Constant Faith with a New View

Jean B. Burden

TEL Publishing

Huntersville, NC

For multiple copies or for further information, please contact:

Jean Burden at lilymom7@gmail.com

Copyright © 2016 by Jean B. Burden

Cover Design: Stephen Lursen Art

Cover Photo: Jean B. Burden

Published by: TEL Publishing

Print ISBN: 978-0-9910989-9-6

Scripture taken from the New International Version® unless otherwise noted.

Scripture taken from the Holy Bible, New International Version®, NIV®, Copyright © 1973, 1978, 1984, 2011 by Biblica, Inc., ™. Used by permission of Zondervan. All rights reserved worldwide. www.zondervan.com The "NIV" and "The New International Version" are Trademarks registered in the United States Patent and Trademark Office by Biblica, Inc., ™

Scripture quotations from the Holman Scripture quotations marked HCSB®, are taken from the Holman Christian Standard Bible®, Copyright © 1999, 2000, 2002, 2003, 2009 by Holman Bible Publishers. Used by permission. HCSB® is a federally registered trademark of Holman Bible Publishers.

Scripture quotations from THE MESSAGE. © by Eugene H. Peterson 1993, 1994, 1995, 1996, 2000, 2001, 2002. Used by permission of Tyndale House Publishers, Inc.

Scripture quotations are taken from the Holy Bible, New Living Translation, copyright ©1996, 2004, 2007, 2013, 2015 by Tyndale House Foundation. Used by permission of Tyndale House Publishers, Inc., Carol Stream, Illinois 60188. All rights reserved.

Library of Congress Cataloging-in-Publication Data

Burden, Jean B., 1958 –

Reflections from the pond: constant faith with a new view

Library of Congress Control Number: 2016952572

Dedication

This book is dedicated to my husband, Dan, for having the vision to move us to Boggy Road, the place God prepared for us.

It is also dedicated to my grandchildren; let this book and my life be a legacy for you to know my deep love for God and my passionate love for you.

LORD, YOU ARE MY PORTION
and my cup of blessing;
You hold my future.
The boundary lines have fallen for me
in pleasant places;
indeed, I have a beautiful inheritance.

(Psalm 16: 5-6 Holman Christian Standard Bible)

Acknowledgments

With special thanks:

To my editor and friend, Terry Lursen, for his willingness to work with me again, even though I'm such a novice.

To my children, grandchildren, husband, friends, and pets, who have been the stories behind the words.

To those who bought my first book and made me realize that with God's help, I could do this again.

Introduction

Let me open with a warning: I am not a trained Bible scholar nor an expert on all matters spiritual. What I am is a daughter of God, wholly and completely dedicated to write what He nudges me to write, sing what He nudges me to sing, say what He nudges me to say, and do everything He tells me to do. Everything. Even write a book!

Quite a number of years ago, God used someone else's book to impress upon me that I need more than just church and religion; I needed an ongoing, deep relationship with my Father and Savior. From that day until this one, I have continued to grow that relationship and deepen my knowledge of God through study and prayer.

At some time during this growth, God encouraged me to write, always giving me the topic through simple things I saw and experienced around me while walking out this journey called life. I never once imagined writing a book. I simply posted my writings on Facebook, and God used other Christian friends to say, "You really need to publish a book." And so in 2014, I published my first devotional book, **Reflections from the Parlor**. This book is the second in the devotional series, and the title reflects my new location: **Reflections from the Pond**. A few years ago, my husband had a gigantic dream of owning some property he found. He made an offer, the bank laughed at his amount, and I thought we would move on. But no! My husband offered again, and again we were rejected. Finally, after trusting that God would give it to us if He wanted us to have it, the bank dropped the price . . . to our price. It was a miracle, and today I write, overlooking the biggest, most beautiful pond on the property. Trusting God is just the coolest thing ever.

As you read the pages of this book, I encourage you to take them slowly, maybe reading one a day or every other day, but probably reading just one a week. There are 40 devotionals here simply because that is the number God gave me to share. 40 days in the desert, 40 years in the wilderness, 40 days and nights of rain as Noah trusted God. The number just seemed right and perfect, and so there are 40. Take them slowly, and use the scriptures built into the writing or given at the end of each piece as a place of study and meditation. Let those words --- God's words ---speak into your spirit, asking the Holy Spirit to guide you into all truth as you ponder them and how they apply to your life.

I pray that you will be blessed by spending time with me on this journey from our pond on Boggy Road. I also pray that in spending time in meditation, study, and prayer, you will see how God can use you and your destiny to glorify Him and further His kingdom. My journey with Him in the last two years has been busy and exciting, but always, I have managed to slow down and reflect from the pond. I pray you will find reflection here as well.

Be blessed,

Jean Burden

September, 2016

Contents

Waiting on a Baby

November 22, 2014, was a momentous day for our family. After traveling all day by car and planes, my husband, Dan, and I arrived in El Paso, Texas, to spend Thanksgiving with our daughter, Meredith, and her family. Four-year –old Olivia and I did the movie scene: we ran into each other's arms with pure excitement and joy after not seeing each other for over four months, and then she said, "Grandma, I'm going to be a big sister and we're moving back to South Carolina!"

Whoa. Two blessings so big that I couldn't even have imagined receiving them both in the same moment. Needless to say, I cried and cheered. I hugged my daughter and her precious husband. And then, I thanked God for giving our family more than we could possibly imagine, and He did it in such an unexpected way. I love it when He does that . . . surprising us in ways that take our breath away. I indeed was breathless.

And of course, there's a lesson in this moment: we must continue to ask God to bless us and then thank Him both quietly and explosively when He accomplishes things that are so good that we can hardly take it in. We must give Him the glory and the credit, and we must understand that, just like an earthly father, He does it because He hungers to bless us and draw us even closer to Him. Wow . . . He is so good. But there is another lesson in this happy story.

After we shared the news with the family, the other granddaughters became quite giddy and excited about a new cousin. Two of them, Lily and Harper, are only 3 and 2 years old, respectively, and they, of course, wanted to see the baby immediately. ☺ But then in a few days, I observed something fascinating.

Lily and Harper came to my house to visit, heading to the playroom to do some pretending. They were playing "Mommy-Daddy" with my older son's Raggedy Ann and Andy dolls. This was joy enough, considering that those dolls are over 30 years old and were hand made for Asher, but what Lily did next stopped me in awe. She said, "Grandma, I'm going to have a baby."

"You are?" I responded. "Just like Aunt Meredith, huh?"

"Yeah," she said, and then she sat quietly in the rocking chair, being incredibly still. I watched her for a few minutes, and then I said, "Are you okay?

"Yes, Grandma. I'm waiting. Waiting for the baby."

She had the most serious look on her face that any 3-year old could possibly possess, and she sat so still, not moving a muscle. A couple minutes later, she got up and announced that the baby had arrived, and the moment was over. But here's what God spoke to my heart.

Somehow Lily knew, in that sweet moment, that a baby's arrival is about waiting, and this reminds me of Christ. In this busy world we so often live on the run, never sitting still and waiting for Jesus. Waiting for Him to speak to us. Waiting for Him to simply love us. Waiting at the foot of the Cross or the edge of the manger. Waiting for whatever He has in store for us. Just waiting.

Sometimes we are waiting for answers, but in our haste, was ask Him for guidance and then run ahead of Him before He can order our steps. Sometimes we are waiting to be loved, but we run to other places, straight into danger zones orchestrated by Satan, when we could have found the only love worth having by waiting at Jesus' feet. Sometimes we are waiting for forgiveness when it was there all the time; all we had to do was ask.

Waiting. Lily, in her sweet and beautifully simplistic way knew she needed to wait on that baby, and we could learn a lot from that moment. I happen to be writing this during the first week of Advent 2014. Advent is a season of waiting . . . waiting to celebrate the birth of a Savior who completely turned the world and its thinking upside down. The world had been waiting for a King for such a long time, and God, in His surprising, take-our-breath away style, sent a baby to be our King. Only God could do it this way, sending His only Son to redeem our lives. Only God.

And so today, spend at least a few minutes simply speaking to this "only God" and then waiting on Him. I love to sit in my parlor and call out His name, Emmanuel --- God with us --- and then listen for His voice. He is waiting there to love me, forgive me, and bless me in ways that are beyond my imagination, and He wants to do the same for you. Let Him bless you today and in the days to come. Let Him heal your heart of anything that might keep you from a full relationship with Him. Let Him fill you with His grace and mercy and love, bringing beauty from the ashes of your life. And then? Just like we are enjoying the blessings of our new grandbaby on the way and their anticipated move back home, allow yourself to bask in the glow of God's amazing grace. Ask

Him to bless you and then **let Him do it**. You will never be sorry.

"**God can do anything, you know --- far more than you could ever imagine or guess or request in your wildest dreams! He does it not by pushing us around but by working within us, His spirit deeply and gently within us. Glory to God in the church! Glory to God in the Messiah, Jesus! Glory to God down all the generations! Glory through all the millennia! Oh, yes!**"   (Ephesians 3: 20-21, The Message)

The Silent Instruction of Creation

Psalm 19:7 says, "The instruction of the Lord is perfect, renewing one's life; the testimony of the Lord is trustworthy, making the inexperienced wise." (HCSB)

This is a great verse and a comforting promise, but what makes it all the more special is what comes before it (vs. 1-4): "The heavens declare the glory of God; the skies proclaim the work of His hands. Day after day they pour out speech; night after night, they communicate knowledge. There is no speech; there are no words; their voice is not heard. Their message has gone out to all the earth and their words to the ends of the world."

This instruction that is addressed is verse 7 is the lessons that come from God's creation, *not* from His words. There *are* no words because, in Creation, words are not needed. The instruction from the heavens is perfect, renewing one's life, and the testimony from Creation is trustworthy and can make the inexperienced wise.

So let's think about this for a moment. Perfect instruction: what is it we learn from the heavens? We learn consistency. The sun comes up every day; the moon is there every night. The seasons change in their perfect pattern, and none of this ever fails. So, we learn about God's consistency and faithfulness through His creation.

It also says it renews one's life. Doesn't the sun renew our lives and our spirits? Even science has told us that sun provides Vitamin D, which is critical for our moods. The sun renews the earth, which in turn renews our bodies through the things that live and grow on the earth. And the moon? Well, it simply renews my spirit. I love to watch the changing moon over time, knowing that God is always there, in the dark, watching over us, just like "Mr. Moon," as my grandchildren say.

Then it says this: the testimony of Creation can make the inexperienced wise. First, that reminds me that children get one of
their very first lessons about God from witnessing the heavens
and the earth. They show God's mighty hand and prove His day
to day sufficiency and faithfulness. Even children who are not
receiving trustworthy, consistent guidance and love from adults
around them can look at the heavens and see that God created
something amazing that never changes. He is worthy of our love,
even when humans are not. And then there's the rest of us.

Even when we are "inexperienced" in our knowledge of God, we
can also look into the heavens and the earth and witness something greater than we can understand, something comforting in
its faithfulness, and something of more beauty than we can truly
describe.

So today and tonight and tomorrow when you look at the sky,
ponder Creation, and witness the beauty of the earth, let it all in-
struct you perfectly in the ways and Sovereignty of Almighty God.

Seeing the Evidence

I love to watch "Criminal Minds," as they manage to catch the killers because evidence is always left behind. Even the smartest offenders leave some small trace of evidence, especially when they are very careful not to do so.

My grandchildren leave evidence behind, too.

My daughter, Whitney, has a key to my house, and often she will visit with her children, even if I am not home. She might come for a change of scenery, a chance to pick grapes and tomatoes from the garden, or to let her two precious girls swim. And every time they have been in my home, I find evidence of their visit . . . sweet evidence that makes me smile. This morning was one of those times.

As I walked through the house to start my day, I noticed toys out of place. They had done some building with Legos and had played in the indoor playroom, evidenced by the stuffed animals and babies strewn around the room. And they had painted. Lily is three years old, and Harper is two, so their paintings are free and colorful. No lines, no restrictions. They splash the empty white pages with color, and lots of it. They mix colors and paint flowers that are as abstract as Picasso, and their artwork is beautiful. I love to find their creations, and I can even hear their expressions of pride in their work.

"Look, Momma, a fwower!" is how Harper would say it. "Grandma, look at my painting," Lily would say.

This is the evidence of children at play, evidence of creativity and joy. I love finding evidence of their visits, and it's got me thinking: are we, as Christians, leaving enough evidence in our paths that people know when we have been somewhere?

Christians should stand out in the world, leaving evidence of

God's love everywhere we go. When I say "stand out," I don't mean we should be making a scene or being loud about sharing God's love necessarily. We can love people quietly but faithfully. We can love them in a hospital room when we visit to pray. We can love them in the line at Wal-Mart, sharing smiles and kind words and maybe even some financial help. We can love in our neighborhoods, helping those in need until they wonder why, and then we get to share the story of our beautiful Savior. We can be kind in long lines at the DMV, encouraging others to be patient as well. We can share from our overflowing gardens or share our time to help others in need. We can, in the words of a favorite poem, "leave the world a bit better," evidence that we have been in a place and sought to do God's will.

Evidence that we live differently and love differently because God first loved us.

So my question today is this: if you and I were thrown into a "Criminal Minds" episode, but instead of looking for a killer, they were looking for a Savior, would there be enough evidence to convict us? Would they have to dig deeply to find that evidence, or would it be apparent all over our lives that we live and love radically because of Christ?

As you travel your neighborhoods and your cities, leave a trail of evidence behind you . . . a trail of kindness, compassion, justice, generosity, and love.

In the words of a favorite song:

"Let it be said of us, that the Lord was our passion.

That with gladness we bore every cross we were given,

That we fought the good fight, that we finished the course,

Knowing within us the power of the risen Lord.

Let the Cross be our glory, and the Lord be our Song,

By mercy made holy, by the Spirit made strong.

Let the Cross be our glory, and the Lord be our Song,

And the likeness of Jesus be through us made known.

Let the Cross be our glory and the Lord be our Song."

---Steve Fry

Evidence of a life lived for God. I want to be found guilty.

Micah 6:8,

But he's already made it plain how to live, what to do,

   what GOD is looking for in men and women.

It's quite simple: Do what is fair and just to your neighbor,

   be compassionate and loyal in your love,

And don't take yourself too seriously—

   take God seriously.

The Dangerous Dream

Every now and then I have a dream that seems to have a message. In the wee hours of this morning, I had just such a dream, and though it gave *me* a word, I also thought you might need to hear this, too.

In the dream, I was back in a house that looked very much like my mother's home. I had warning . . . not sure from where . . . that two different people who were dangerous to me would be trying to get inside the house. The first one never materialized, but the second danger did indeed show up on the front porch. He was a young, teenage boy, and I'm not sure why he was such a danger, but I know that I was very afraid. I locked every door, secured the dead bolts and slide locks, and stayed away from the windows. Then I headed to the phone to call 911, but in the middle of giving them my address, someone appeared out of nowhere. She was the boy's mother, and she stopped the call, proceeding to tell me why he *wasn't* a danger. She would handle him. At that point, I awoke and shrugged off the unusual dream until a little later. But during my prayer time, I felt a nudge to rethink what this might mean.

Recently I've been battling some old temptations . . . thorns in my side where I have failed God repeatedly. I have struggled quite a bit with why I cannot seem to find consistent victory in these areas, and just yesterday, I believe that God placed two perfectly timed sermons within my hearing to send me a message: I can resist any temptation because God provides a way out. God. Not me. God. I don't have to do this in my own power.

And so the dream...as I asked God what this dream might be teaching me, it became so clear. The dangers in the dream represent the areas where I've been under attack by Satan. One was "out there" but never really showed itself except through my concern, and doesn't Satan do that? He wants to get us all worked up about something that won't even happen, and when we allow him to do that, we lose our peace.

The second danger --- the boy on the porch --- was there and obvious to me, and I was afraid. But in my fear, I knew what to do: call out for help. I called 911 in my dream, but in reality, we always have God right there, waiting to give us a way out. We just need to call out to Him. He wants to provide a way out of the dangers of temptation and fear; we just have to trust that He is there and ready to save us through His strength, not our own.

As far as the boy on the porch? Sometimes the things Satan throws at us are obvious temptations to sin. We've been there and done that, and so, we recognize the danger and even know what to do: call for help. But sometimes, like the other danger, Satan can be sneaky and come at us with something we don't even recognize as a problem, and that's when we can find ourselves afraid even though we should be at peace. And yet, the solution is the same: lock the doors with God's Word and with prayer to protect ourselves and provide the armor of God around us so Satan has no power.

One more lesson: we must armor ourselves daily . . . even hourly

. . . to prepare for battle. Soldiers don't wait until they are *in* the battle to figure out how to win. They train, keep their weapons ready to fire, and mentally prepare for the fight. We must do the same, and it involves a few simple but powerful training methods.

1) **Live in God's Word.** Seek verses that address your particular temptations and commit them to your heart and mind. They will serve you well when Satan tries to throw you under the bus. Jesus is the perfect model for this. When Satan tempted Him in the desert, He came back with God's Word.

2) **Live in constant communication with God.** He can't help us much if we never talk to Him, asking for His strength and power in the dangerous situations of our lives, and if we never listen to His voice and guidance through the Holy Spirit. Make time to pray. Notice the verb: **MAKE.** It doesn't happen by accident. Make time for God and you will live in His peace and strength.

3) **Recognize your enemy.** The quicker you recognize Satan's plans to destroy you, the faster you will have victory.

One last thing . . . if Satan is on the attack, know this: he needs to shut you down when he is afraid of what you are preparing to accomplish for God's kingdom. He needs to defeat you when you are a light against his darkness. He cannot afford to let you win when your winning means people are coming to Christ. So be prepared, and I will do the same. Scripture says that Satan comes at us like a roaring lion, seeking to steal, kill, and destroy.

Okay. We know it, and we know what to do about it. Come back at Him with the strength of Almighty, Sovereign God and the power of a risen Savior.

Us: 1   Satan 0. Game over.

Chainsaw Power

I once heard a pastor tell the story of a man who went to the hardware store and bought a chain saw. He was quite excited because his friends had told him that it would make his work of cutting trees so much easier. He took that chain saw home and immediately set himself to work, but in no time at all, he was frustrated. He didn't seem to be making any progress, and the trees surely weren't falling. So back to the store he went to complain about this ineffective tool. He took the chain saw into the store and told the owner that it simply didn't work. The owner asked to see the chain saw, pulled the starter cord, and listened to it run. The man was shocked: he told the owner, "I didn't know I had to pull that cord. I've just been sawing back and forth and nothing has been happening." Stupid story? Maybe not. The man had power in his hands and he didn't even recognize it. Are we so different?

As Christians we are promised power and authority based on the name of Jesus, and yet most days we live without ever pulling the cord on the chain saw. We pray but not expectantly. We ask but not boldly. We beg but don't thank God for the answer before it comes. And sometimes we simply don't ask at all, fearful that God doesn't want to hear our petitions, but He does. In Mark 11, verses 22-24 (NIV), the Bible says this: "'Have faith in God,' Jesus answered. 'I tell you the truth, if anyone says to this mountain, 'Go, throw yourself into the sea,' and does not doubt in his heart but believes what he says will happen, it will be done for him. Therefore, I tell you, whatever you ask for in prayer, believe that you have received it and it will be yours.'" Powerful verbs of authority. Let's take a look at them for just a moment.

Have faith. We must have faith in God, not in ourselves and our human abilities but in God's ability to do the impossible. When we bring even a little faith to the Lord, we find that He is all-sufficient to meet our every need.

Do not doubt. It's so easy to ask and then slip into doubt because we are human, and we know *we* are unable to do the impossible, but God relishes in doing the impossible. We must trust him and not doubt; He will answer and then *He* will be glorified in our lives.

Believe. Look back over the course of your life. Remember the times God has answered you in the past. Let it be your reminder to believe Him again today, no matter the gravity of your current situation.

Ask in prayer. Don't call your friend and ask. Don't call your boss and ask. Ask *God* in prayer for your deepest needs and your simplest concerns. He loves us and is waiting to bless us. We simply must ask.

When I was growing up in the church, we often sang "There's Power in the Blood," and until a few years ago, I never really gave that song much thought. But the truth is this: there *is* power in the blood --- the blood of Jesus. The blood that He shed on the Cross has the power to save us from our sinfulness. The blood that He shed on the Cross has the power to redeem all mankind.

The blood of Jesus takes sinful, hopeless people and washes us whiter as snow. That same power is available to us today in our lives, and yet we often fail to pray with the authority of the blood. Do you want power in your life? Pray the blood of Jesus over every situation that would discourage and defeat you. Satan has no power against the blood of Jesus, and with that prayer in place, the mountain of defeat that he throws at us will be tossed into the sea. I like to think it drowns in the depths of the Atlantic, never to be seen again.

In the New Testament, Jesus gave a bunch of fishermen the authority and power to heal and preach in His name. They weren't any more special than you and I, and they had no more gifts than we do. What they had, we have as well: the authority of Jesus Christ, our Savior. Today don't pray wimpy prayers. Pray boldly, knowing that God is waiting to hear you and meet you where you are. Pray with authority, asking Him to hold to His promises to protect us with His wings. Pull the cord on your chain saw so that trees of doubt fall before you and you live a life of power in Christ.

Hebrews 10: 19-22 , "Therefore, brothers and sisters, since we have confidence to enter the Most Holy Place by the blood of Jesus, by a new and living way opened for us through the curtain, that is, his body, and since we have a great priest over the house of God, let us draw near to God with a sincere heart and with the full assurance that faith brings, having our hearts sprinkled to cleanse us from a guilty conscience and having our bodies washed with pure water."

1 John 5: 14-15, "This is the confidence we have in approaching God: that if we ask anything according to his will, he hears

us. And if we know that he hears us – whatever we ask – we know that we have what we asked of him."

Ephesians 3: 20-21, "Now to him who is able to do immeasurably more than all we ask or imagine, according to his power that is at work within us, to him be glory in the church and in Christ Jesus throughout all generations, for ever and ever! Amen."

A Hopeless Flower Bed

One of the tasks with which I have a love-hate relationship every spring is that of taking back my flower beds from the weeds. It never fails that the weeds, vines, and thorns get in there before I get a chance to be on spring break, and once there, they get a strangle hold. Every year it seems to get worse, and this year, I finally gave up on one of my most precious beds. It was the first raised bed that my carpenter husband built for me years ago, and I loaded it with incredibly beautiful daylilies . . . some of my very finest ones. But the vines have won the battle, and just this week, I removed everything that deserves to be saved; sadly, I am going to destroy the rest. Sad story of a favorite spot in my yard, but God was good to give me a word while I worked, salvaging my precious flowers from the ravages of the weeds.

When we become Christians and start a fresh new life found in Christ, we are like that pristine bed when it was first planted: clean and beautiful. God has forgiven us and washed us in the blood of Christ --- we are clean. But what often happens over time is that we allow little dangers to slip into our lives – little dangers like not praying, not reading God's Word, slipping into what we consider to be "small" sins, or allowing ourselves to spend Sundays in ways other than worshiping our Father. And with every day, every month, every year that we allow ourselves to fall away from the source of our strength, the "weeds" of life take over, growing more vicious with every day that we don't fight back with the spiritual disciplines we know will keep up strong. And eventually, our situation, like my flower bed, looks hopeless . . . good only for destruction and weed killer.

But Jesus Christ...

We only need to say the name and call on Him for help, and we can immediately find ourselves running back to Him to once again be washed in His blood. The very blood that dripped from His body from the scourging. The very blood that poured from the wounds in His hands and feet. The very blood that was sacrificed so we are never hopeless. Jesus Christ gave everything --- His love, His seat in heaven, and His very body and blood --- to save us from the weeds and thorns in our lives. We are made pristine again through His blood, and His righteousness is credited to us. It's hard to fathom, but yes, He did *that much* for us on the Cross.

And, there's more.

I pulled out my new pressure washer this morning, pretty excited to have something in my hands with that kind of power. I thought it would be an easy task, but years of grime do not let go without a fight, and so my power tool and I both worked tediously to clean the deck, outdoor furniture and siding on the house. The analogy of Jesus continues. When we come to Him, he washes us clean, but we still carry old dirty habits that, created over many years, are not transformed overnight. It takes prayer and a complete surrender into the arms of God the Father and Christ the Son. And the truth is that our deep metamorphosis will take time. Time and prayer and God's Word. But at the end, our lives will be transformed in unimaginable ways, and like my deck furniture that looks better than ever, we will be a more beautiful version of our former selves.

So as you clean, pulling the weeds from your yard and washing the dirt from your deck, remember Christ, who accepts us as we are and then holds our hands as we rid ourselves of the weeds of sin. It's the best spring cleaning ever!

Braveheart and Some Good Theology

It might surprise some of you who don't know me so well to find out that my taste in movies is, well . . . a little intense. I love a great story of suspense combined with love, revenge, passion, and just enough blood to keep it real. "Braveheart" is one of my top 3 of all time, and I have watched it over and over, never failing to be captured by the story of William Wallace, a man who lived a passionate life for family, friends, and country. The evil Longshanks had Wallace's wife killed, and in that one act, he set off rebellion the likes of which I'm sure he wished he had never seen. You see, Wallace was a man of passion: he loved deeply . . . his wife, his country, and a future of freedom from tyranny. I love him for his passion, and so I watch again and again. There is one scene that hasn't left my mind lately, and I think there is some theological truth in it if we look at it in terms of God.

When Longshanks is on the warpath to kill Wallace, Longshanks' beautiful daughter-in-law, whose own life is a sham of an arranged marriage to his homosexual son, has fallen in love with Wallace. In one scene in which she has risked her own life to carry vital information to Wallace, we hear these lines:

William Wallace: Why do you help me?

Princess Isabelle: Because of the way you are looking at me now.

That's where I can't tear my mind away from God.

Lately in my own life, I've been facing some really difficult situations, and through everything, God has been here. He has been faithful, and He has delivered me and my family over and over. He has never failed to let me feel His presence, and in my prayers, I have found myself saying to God, "Why do you help me?" I surely don't deserve it; I haven't earned it; and I can never repay Him for all He has done for me. So again, I ask, "God, why do You help me?" And His answer is always the same in my spirit: "Because of the way you are looking at me now."

Now I don't want to get into trouble with my more knowledgeable friends, so let me be very clear: I know that God loved me even before He formed me in the womb. He loved me long before I fell in love with Him, and He sacrificed His only Son so you and I could be forgiven and free. But I also know another truth: scripture says that when we delight in the Lord, He hears our prayers and He will give us the desires of our hearts. And when I look at God, I delight in Him every single day, simply because He is God, my Father, and He loved me first. I didn't always feel this way, but I do today. I am passionately in love with our giant-slaying, stone-rolling, bush-burning, veil-tearing God! And it pleases Him when I delight in Him! He has used my passion for Him to turn *my* desires into *His* desires; He has changed my heart, and I know that He celebrates when I fall to my knees or walk in the beauty of a spring day, all the while declaring my love for Him, the only Master of the Universe. (A little aside there for my two boys)

Again, today and tomorrow and the next day, I will ask, "God, why do You help me?" I pray that you will ask Him the same question. Let Him answer you with His great love. Let Him answer you by pouring His blessings into your life. Let Him answer you by re-minding you that He loves it when you love Him with unbridled passion, making Him the focus of your existence. Make Him your magnificent obsession, and watch Him show off with His amazing grace and mighty power over your life . . . the same power that raised Jesus from the dead on resurrection morning.

William Wallace changed a country because of his passionate love. God changed the whole world for eternity. Today, I will look on Him with eyes that show my adoration and my humility at being privileged to be a child of the King! Join me in loving Him and sharing His love with everyone whose life can be changed by a Savior. We have been passed over by the Death Angel and have been given new life in Christ; pass it on!

Don't Be a Dying Ember

I was a public school teacher for 34 years. That's a long time to survive and thrive in a profession where, for many years, isolation was the norm. My first teaching assignment placed me in a portable building with no phone, no intercom and no support system. I was out there alone, trying to survive every day with nothing. I was a first-year teacher, and I can tell you most assuredly that the only reason I stayed in the profession was that God had a plan for me. Staying was horrible and not at all logical, but stay I did. (I had to eat!) My next position was not much better, and again I was left isolated and alone, trying to figure out by myself what was best for the troubled children in my care. I was in another portable building without the benefit of the expertise in the main building. I planned alone. I taught alone. And, I survived alone. Survived . . . but I didn't grow. Teaching is not supposed to be an isolated profession, and yet for years, educators were given a key to a room and left to figure it out. Today in our best schools, thank goodness, that doesn't happen anymore. In fact, in my school, collaboration is the expectation because we know that when we share best practices and listen to each other, we all grow from the experience. I will never work in isolation again, which brings me to an important point: as Christians, it is almost impossible to grow and develop our spiritual maturity in isolation.

A local pastor, Dr. Jeff Gaskins, spoke on this concept recently, and he shared a story about a man who quit going to church. His pastor visited him and used an object lesson to make his point: he took one coal from a burning fire and watched as it fizzled out, turning to ashes. Without a word, the man got the message - we need to be surrounded by "burning coals" to keep our faith alive. Without being surrounded regularly by the family of God, we are in danger of losing the "heat" in our faith and dying out. But there's hope.

There are churches everywhere, waiting to welcome you with open arms and Christian fellowship. I have visited more in the last year than I can count, but after much praying, God placed my new faith home in my path. I found love, acceptance, great lessons in Bible study and worship, and wonderful Christian brothers and sisters who care about my faith walk. They reached out to me, and they answered a need we all have: to be accepted and loved. Being in a church fellowship also answers a need for us to be connected to others who love what we love and desire what we desire. It gives us a place to use our God-given talents for His kingdom and work with others who are already invested in God's plan. You see, I want to serve, but re-inventing the wheel is daunting. Being in a strong, missions-based fellowship provides the opportunity to plug into what God is already doing through like-minded believers. What joy! I don't have to work alone, study alone, or stand alone! But don't misunderstand me: there are many facets of my faith that happen in the quiet of my home. I write alone, I pray alone, and I read Scripture alone. But when I combine those disciplines with a fellowship of other believers who hunger for God and live to worship Him, I find accountability, love, and joy. I also know that my spiritual growth happens by leaps and bounds.

So today if you're telling yourself that you can worship at home . . . that you don't ever need to go to church, please reconsider. Ask God what He would have you do. Ask a good friend to go to church with you. Find a church fellowship that puts worship, missions, and God's Word first. Find a fellowship that loves *ALL people*, one that takes the mandate of Jesus seriously: love God and love others. Immerse yourself in the family of God. You just might have the time of your life!

Competing for My Lap

If you've read my writings before, you know about my beautiful Belle, my yellow lab. She is a loving, sweet dog who craves my attention first thing every morning. She sits at my feet and paws my lap if I don't rub her head and give her a good morning scratch. But now there's a small issue, she has competition. Belle had a beautiful litter of black lab puppies last year, and we decided to keep the liveliest of the litter. The pup's name is Eliza, named after Eliza Doolittle from *My Fair Lady*. The name is a perfect fit because our Eliza is much like the human version, needing lots of refinement and education.   My husband, Dan, has worked with her, and her manners are much better now! She sits to wait on her breakfast, she is much calmer, and she knows how to retrieve a duck, but there's one area in which she is a pushy little girl: wanting my lap. She and Belle both try their best to get into my lap at once, and if Eliza sees Belle head my way, she piles into the mix, competing to get a rub and some love. They can be quite overwhelming at times. This morning, when Eliza wasn't getting enough of my attention away from Belle, she nipped me on my side! Needless to say, I paid attention then! If they only knew that my love is big enough always for both of them, they wouldn't need to compete.

The same is true with God.

In the world we often feel like my dogs: we are constantly jock-eying for a position with people we desire to impress or please or simply to be in relationship with. But, it's different with God. He has enough love and a big enough "lap" for all of us. Every one of us. Every single day. His love is so wide and deep and immeasur-able that it's hard for us wrap our heads around just how much He loves us. And because God's love is so all-encompassing, we don't have to compete at all. There is more than enough for all of us, and He wants ALL of us in relationship with Him.

But there's another point, too. Eliza is a rather destructive little girl. She tears up plants, pots, neighbors' trinkets that are left un-guarded, and even my outdoor furniture. You would think I would be so angry with her, but I'm not. I get frustrated, but I under-stand Eliza: she is a typical puppy, and chewing is what puppies do. Well, we are typical humans: sinners --- and sinning is what we do. And so God not only loves us even when we sin, but He also provided a way for our sins to be forgiven: He gave us His Son, Jesus. In John 3:16-17, we read that God loved us so much --- *ALL* of us --- that He gave us His only Son, and we simply must believe in Him to be saved. It also goes on to say that Jesus didn't come into the world to condemn us; He came to save us *without* condemnation. What an amazing gift! He did for us what we could never do for ourselves, and there's one more thing.

With every day of training and correction, Eliza becomes more like the grown-up dog we want her to be. This is exactly what God wants for us: He wants us to read His word – our training; pray for forgiveness, discernment and guidance – our correction; and become more like He wants us to be with every passing moment. And what does He want us to be? Like Jesus. He sent His Son, giving us the perfect model for how we are to live and love and serve while we are walking this earthly journey. He gave us the words of Jesus in the Bible and the words of others who knew Him, walked with Him, and loved Him. He also gave us the privilege of prayer, a practice in which we learn more about the heart of God and His plans for our lives, and He has great plans for us . . . plans that are immeasurably more than we can ask or think, which brings me to one last thought.

Very soon, Dan and I are moving to our retirement property. We already spend time down there, but living there is going to be amazing. It's peaceful and quiet, and we will be surrounded by the beauty of God's earth and sky. Eliza and Belle already love the place, but when we move to our new home, they can stay forever, free to run and swim and play all day every day. It will be the perfect life for my two beautiful girls. So far, they only get a glimpse of that life as we visit, but then we always have to leave. But very soon, life will be immeasurably greater than they could possibly imagine, and they will be living life at full capacity for a couple of Labrador retrievers: free to run and enjoy God's bounty.

God wants this for all of us, too. He wants us to settle into His arms and live this life surrounded by His love, His goodness, and His mercy, and nothing could be better than this. Today, right now, ask God to bless you indeed. Trust His incomparable love. Allow yourself to appreciate the beauty and bounty of a life lived in relationship with God... the one who has enough love for all of us.

Seeing All I've Missed

This morning I decided to power walk to our new house site. It turned out to be a battle with the deer flies, and I lost, but that's another issue. On the way, I reached a stretch where there are few houses and mostly trees, and some things caught my eye . . . some beautiful trees I have never noticed and a couple of cottage-like houses that were quiet in the early morning light. Now, I have driven this road for the last three years and never paid attention to these things. Why? Because I am always in my car where the view is limited and somewhat obscured, and I am on a mission to reach my end destination. Both of these factors have kept me from noticing blessings that have been there all along. And this reminds me of a lesson I heard once about Abraham.

When God promised Abraham that he would be the father of many nations, it seemed impossible. Absolutely, ridiculously impossible. He simply could not fathom that God could use him in his old age to father the nations, and one pastor I heard said it this way: he was in his tent, pondering God's promise, and he needed to get *out* of the tent to see what God had in store. When he stepped out of his tent, God was able to show him . . . not just tell him . . . that his descendants would be as numerous as the stars in the sky. Hearing that promise sounds good, but seeing those innumerable stars is breathtaking, and Abraham was able to believe. Sounds like my morning, doesn't it?

I have been "in my tent" so long that I've forgotten to step out-side and see the gifts that God has so graciously provided. I tend to see and appreciate those gifts at the house site itself, and I am overwhelmed by His goodness, but it's in the journey to that place that I miss so much of what He has created. And just like Abraham, God has shown me to step outside my tent and look around, seeing His abundance and goodness. But that's not all.

He has reminded me to slow down...way down. When I am in a hurry to reach my final destination, I miss so much along the way that I can't appreciate the blessings He has left in my path. Life as a whole is like this, too. When we are in such a hurry to reach end destinations in life, we miss the joy of the daily journey. We rush to the weekend, to summer, to retirement, to the next "end game," and we fail to notice the little joys of the journey . . . joys like breathtaking nature, the laughter of children, the glistening pond, the friend who needs and loves us, and the list goes on and on. As I write this, we are building a new home, one in which we will spend the rest of our earthly lives, and I am stopping to enjoy and be amazed by every single step. Just this week, I watched a powerful crane lift the roof trusses into place and held my breath as builders stood on nails while balancing those trusses. Amaz-ing. I will watch and chronicle every step so when we are living there, I can truly appreciate all that went into this new home. And there's one more thing . . . God just gave me a moment about those deer flies.

Life will always throw distractions our way. Count on it. The deer flies of life, the mosquitoes on our path, and the yellow jackets will do everything they can to steal our attention from what is most important, but we don't have to let them win.   There are products on the market to keep them off our skin and other products designed to kill them in their tracks, and so we have another lesson. We have God's word with us every minute to stop the distractions and destroy the efforts of the enemy. Remember what scripture says in John 10:10, "...the thief (the enemy) comes to steal, kill and destroy..." but we have weapons to defeat the enemy . . . weapons of prayer, praise, and God's holy word. If we prepare well and refuse to be distracted by the "deer flies" of life, we don't have to lose our focus. We can enjoy every moment of our journey as we head toward an end destination of eternal life with God. This is a no-brainer for me, and I pray it is for you. Choose to *enjoy* the journey, *appreciate* God's abundant blessings, and *know* that you never travel alone. It just doesn't get better than this.

Broken and Ground

Yesterday I watched my younger lab, Eliza, chew on a piece of a deer's antlers. She's been working on it for some time . . . weeks, in fact . . . and as I thought of her this morning, I understood something about myself. There are some thoughts to which I keep returning, chewing on them and turning them over and over in my mind. One of those recent "bones" is concerning my responsibility to love others, but more than that, it's about my desire to love openly and in the words of a local church slogan, "Do something about it."

A number of years ago, God gave me a phrase. He didn't say it out loud, but it had to come from Him because I surely could not have made it up. I was seated at a long table with other women who were serving in the Seaside Emmaus community. We had some down time (physically), and God used that time to give me the phrase: *Broken and Ground*. I wrote it on a yellow Post-It note and passed it to my friend, Ann. She looked at me with a questioning face, and I didn't know what to say except that God had impressed it upon my heart. I've been chewing on this "bone" ever since that day.

So this morning, these two bones just might be coming together to form the foundation of something He is asking me to do, and this writing is the first step.

After prayer and pondering, here's what I know *Broken and Ground* means. We are all broken. Broken by other people. Broken by life's circumstances. Broken by loss. Broken by our own choices. Broken by friends who have abandoned us. Broken by disappointment in those who were supposed to love and protect us. Broken. But God . . . and with Him, there is always a "but" . . .God can use our brokenness. In fact, scripture promises that He can give us beauty for our ashes. So what about this idea of being *Ground*? Well, coffee is my favorite beverage, and so it's perfectly appropriate and just like God to give me a coffee analogy: when I buy my favorite coffee beans, they don't give out their amazing aroma until they have been ground. And it's the same with our lives. God can take our brokenness, grind it up, and make us fragrant gift offerings to Him and His kingdom. He did it first with His only Son.

"Walk in the way of love, just as Christ loved us and gave himself up for us as a fragrant offering and sacrifice to God" (Ephesians 5:2, NIV)

Jesus' body was broken. He chose that brokenness on our behalf, knowing that His sacrifice would become a fragrant offering to God. *Broken and ground.*

And then there's Mary. We've all read the story of Mary and Martha, and poor old Martha always gets the criticism. (My friend, Patti, says that it makes her mad . . . she is an awesome Martha, and I'm glad she cooks for me!) Anyway, Mary chooses the "better part," sitting at the feet of Christ, and she did something seemingly wasteful: she poured very expensive perfume on His feet. The scripture says this:

"Then Mary took about a pint of pure nard, an expensive per-fume; she poured it on Jesus' feet and wiped his feet with her hair. And the house was filled with the fragrance of the per-fume." (John 12:3)

She was criticized for her gift, but Jesus saw her heart. He knew that she sat before Him to worship Him, to love Him, and to pour a fragrant, sacrificial gift offering on His feet. Her offering was pure and uncontaminated, and our brokenness can be that as well. When we give our brokenness to God as an offering of re-pentance and sacrifice, He can repair us, turning us into a beau-tiful fragrance to impact the world around us. Beauty for ashes. Broken and ground. But it can't stop there.

Notice that I said "a beautiful fragrance to impact the world"? I believe that God takes our brokenness, grinds it up, and makes us fragrant again, not so we can stay quiet about it, but so we can become a fragrant offering to our families, our communities, our churches, and our world. Wherever He asks us to go. If all we do is bask in the fragrance and close our doors to keep it to ourselves, then all we have is healing, but God expects more. He heals us to we can be a part of healing others. He asks us to use our brokenness to reach people who are broken . . . people just like us. He expects a sacrificial and fragrant offering of our lives . . . our time, our money, our talents, and our hearts to "do some-thing about it," whatever "it" He places in our paths.

Which brings me to the thing that keeps chewing on my heart these days: **Division.**

The division we are seeing in the world today is breaking my heart. As a nation, I believe we are moving backward instead of forward, forgetting that our command and joy is to love each other the way Christ first loved us. We are to love beyond our own understanding. We are to love those who have hurt us. We are to love those whose paths are different from our own. We are to love . . . well, everyone. Love crosses racial boundaries, and in all the years of my teaching career, it was the thing that gave me so much joy. Loving children . . . all children of all races and all backgrounds . . . was easy. My earthly parents and my heavenly Father made it easy because they modeled it right before my eyes. And I want to make sure that my sweet community in which I live is loving in just that way. I want every neighborhood to be praying for another neighborhood. I want people to come together from all races because we want a better world for our children and grandchildren. I want to love people so much that I can see God taking the brokenness of our histories and our hearts and grinding them up with complete, unconditional love.

And I want it to start with me.

I don't know what this will look like in the coming days, but I know this: God breaks our hearts for the very things that break His, and division in our communities is breaking His heart. Division and racial hatred are the opposites of what Jesus commanded of us --- not requested but **commanded:**

"A new command I give you: Love one another. As I have loved you, so you must love one another. By this everyone will know that you are my disciples, if you love one another." (John 13: 34-35, NIV)

He spoke these words not long before He died for all of us. Somehow that makes it even more urgent. If I knew that my death was imminent, I would say the most important things to my children, and so Jesus did.

In my community, I want to be known as His. I want it to be clear that I am His disciple, and how will that look? I don't know the details of the plan He is placing before me, but I know that it looks like, feels like, and smells like love.

Broken hearts and broken communities being ground in love, and if we love as He commanded, the fragrance will be amazing!

Pondering Mary

It is the Sunday before Christmas, and as I sit in the dark of the early morning, I am not thinking about the presents I haven't wrapped. I'm not worrying about my Christmas meal. I'm not even worrying about my husband's December 26 birthday present that isn't bought. I'm thinking about Mary, the mother of Jesus.

Take a minute with me to ponder the amazing story of an adolescent that changed history.

First of all, think about her shock as a very young Jewish girl in a world where God had been silent for four centuries. No one had heard from Him in over 400 years, and yet, Mary received a divine message through an angel, a message that would change the course of her life and the future of the entire world. "You are highly favored." Wow. What it must have been like to have heard that message. And isn't it just like God to have brought the first Word in so many years to a common girl?

First lesson: God loves us all, as common as we are, and has a plan for every single one of us.

Secondly, she was told the name to be used for this Holy Child: Jesus. When I was expecting my last son, my husband told me the name, Jake. He said it sounded strong, and we knew that for a child with possible health problems, Jake would need to be strong. God knew exactly what was needed as well. Jesus is transliterated from the Hebrew Yeshu'a --- a common name --- so perfectly planned for a Savior who would save common people like us.

Second lesson: God leaves no detail to chance in sending His Son or planning our lives.

Third, Mary was told that she would be "with child" because, "The Holy Spirit will come upon you, and the power of the Most High will overshadow you." No one else in history has had this happen, and yet it is surely a foreshadowing for all believers. When we accept Christ as our Savior, the Holy Spirit comes into our lives as well. In her book, "Jesus: 90 Days with the One and Only," Beth Moore calls this "the most glorious invasion of privacy that ever graced a human life!" Third lesson: When Jesus left this earthly life, He left us the Holy Spirit to be with us always, and we could not have asked for a greater gift.

Fourth, Mary responded with "yes" and I'm sure plenty of awe. She gave her total commitment and submission to a plan that God chose for her. It couldn't have been easy. She was young, engaged, and alone during the angel's visit. She could have said, "This is too hard. You surely cannot ask this of me." But it's *not* what she said. She responded with complete surrender to God's holy plan, and her surrender changed everything for the rest of us.

Fourth lesson: our surrender to God's plan is almost always about someone else. When we choose to do as we are led by God, we can be used by His hand, with His strength, to be an answer to someone else's prayers.

And finally, take a look what is called Mary's *Magnificat.* Mary's song of praise found in Luke 1: 46-55. She rejoices in her God, proclaiming His greatness and calling herself His humble servant. She knows that she is favored and blessed, and she sings her words to God with the assurance of one who knows she is a part of His great plan. She is still young, still processing the news that is almost unbelievable, and yet, she praises God, the Holy One.

Last lesson: Even in the unexpected circumstances of our lives, we can praise God, and we must always remember that we serve Him as a privilege, with a humble spirit. Rather than asking, "Why me, God? Why would you ask me to do this hard thing?", we must always say: "Yes, God, your humble servant is waiting and praising You for Your great works."

Do you feel like God might be asking you to do a hard thing this year, or next? Look at Mary and her response, and then...

Magnify the Lord!

A Lesson from a Pine

I've never liked pine trees. They make a mess, and it hurts when I pick up the pine cones. They always blow pine straw in aggravating places, and my driveway at our old house was never free of the mess.

But when we moved, I got a fresh perspective and appreciation for pine trees.

One year ago, I created a flower bed under two pine trees that are close together on our new property. This year everything I placed there is thriving! And I mean *really* thriving! As I watered and walked just a bit ago, God gave me a thought: the pine trees are the perfect mix of allowing sun and providing shade. Perfect.

And aren't we like that? I'm sure that sometimes people have looked at me and thought, "Isn't she aggravating? And she leaves a mess everywhere she goes." But just like a pine tree, I have my redeeming qualities, too, and God uses those very qualities to give me purpose as I provide light and shade to those around me. And that pine straw that I always hated? Well, now I harvest my own pine straw for my flower beds. The pine cones are still a challenge, but my granddaughters like to compete to see who can pick up the most. I think I'll let them keep on gathering while I sit back and appreciate the perfection of one of God's great creations.

Thank You, Father, for helping me to see with new eyes.

Jeremiah 29: 11, "For I know the plans I have for you," declares the LORD, "plans to prosper you and not to harm you, plans to give you hope and a future." (NIV)

Ephesians 2:10, "For we are God's handiwork, created in Christ Jesus to do good works, which God prepared in advance for us to do." (NIV)

God's Great Dash

There's a thought I've heard many times after someone's death. When we look at the dash on the tombstone, what does it say about that person's life? How did he or she spend "the dash" in between the years etched on the tombstone? Well, today I got a new perspective on the dash.

I listened to a dear friend, Ann, as she delivered her first sermon at her new church. She was speaking on the unity of the body of Christ and the various gifts with which God equips us as part of the body. But somewhere in there, she said this: "God owns the beginning and the end. He is both Alpha and Omega." Now, I've heard that a million times, but today I sensed something different in my spirit: since God is the beginning and the end, what am I doing in the dash of this world? How am I using the time He allows me during His great "dash"? Granted, His dash is much longer than my personal one, but He expects me to use my dash to be a part of His greater dash. And so, I ask again, what am I doing to change myself, my community and my world during my small portion of His great dash? How am I using the gifts He has entrusted to me to be a part of someone else's destiny?

It's a big question. But here's what I know for sure: God placed me here in a specific time and place, with a chosen family, with a certain skill and gift set, and He expects me to use those gifts to make a difference every single day. And, there's more. He expects me sometimes to go way beyond what I believe I can do; He needs me sometimes just to leap into His arms, trusting Him to catch me and equip me to do whatever He has in store. Do I always feel equipped? Oh no, but His Word promises that if we follow His call, He will give us what we need to accomplish His tasks in His timing. Scary? Not really if we indeed have the faith of a mustard seed. In fact, in Romans 12, we are told that God has distributed a measure of faith to each one of us, so we must put ourselves out there in complete trust.

Which leads me to the last dash I want us to consider: January 1 – December 31. Every January we have a new beginning, a chance to do things both big and small for the 365 days we are granted, assuming we make it to December 31. And so I ask again: what does God have in store for you and me in the next year? How might we use every single day to honor Him so that we can look back at the end of this year and know we ran the good race God planned for us?

If you are not sure what God wants of you in the dash of your life, pray. Read His Word and pray, asking Him to guide your eyes, your ears, and your heart to do the great things He has planned for you. And He *does* have a plan for you because He loves You and He knows the difference you can make. Jeremiah 29:11 says this: "I know the plans I have for you, says the Lord. Plans to prosper you and not harm you, plans to give you a hope and a future." Let His plans fill your dash and let your destiny be about something greater than just living through the days, one to the next. Offer yourself as a living sacrifice to His great and sovereign plan, and when the next year is over, we can hope that He will say, "Well done, my good and faithful servant."

Don't Want to Miss a Thing

Music is a language for me, and often I will get a song stuck in my head. Usually when this happens, God is trying to nudge me to write. The lyrics that won't leave me alone are from Aerosmith's song, "I Don't Want to Miss a Thing." I know you must know that tune and I can bet that you're singing it in your head right now..."'Cause I..." Well, hopefully you know the words and legally I can't print them for copyright purposes, so while you read here in the next few moments, hum that tune with me.

The words of that song talk about surrendering forever to a love that is treasured, a love that is so real that you simply get lost in the other person.

The song talks about a love that, sometimes, keeps you awake at night because you want to be with that person so much so that you don't want to miss anything that you could possibly do together. Are you still singing the tune?

Have you ever loved anyone with the kind of love that you even dream about them and when you awake, the morning can't get going fast enough to see them once again?

Ok, for the sake of this moment, let's agree to apply this kind of loving surrender to God.

As this new year began, I have sung this tune a million times in my head, but every time, I sense myself singing to God: God, I don't want to fall asleep 'cause I don't want to miss a thing. But let's backtrack.

When I was a little girl, the youngest in a family of three girls, I always had trouble going to sleep. I would flip my body, placing my head at the foot of the bed because, in that arrangement, I could listen to my parents' conversations. We lived in a very small house, and my parents' bedroom was down a short hallway, separated only by a cubicle of a bathroom. I could hear their sweet conversations as they lay in bed together, and I always listened because I didn't want to miss a thing. And, there's more.

I hated going to sleep. Hated it. The reason? I always felt like there were great things to do, and sleeping seemed like a colossal waste of time. I was, and still am, an overachiever. I wanted to get on with the business of tomorrow's plans. Sleeping was just a necessary evil. And yet, I have learned a lot about sleeping in the last number of years.

Sleeping is God's way of resting my body and my mind, preparing me for the great things that lie ahead in the new day to come. So thanks be to God, He has changed my attitude about sleeping, but I still wake up, ready to take on the day, to jump into whatever He has in store for my life.

I don't want to miss a thing.

I am writing this at the fresh beginning of a new year, and I feel an urgency in my spirit: I don't want to miss a thing God has ordained for me.

I want to spend my days in "sweet surrender" to His will, staying lost in Him forever. In the words of a favorite song, I want Him to be the "air I breathe," being desperate for Him as I walk through each new day. I want to treasure every single moment He gives me, knowing that every breath is a gift.

My mother died from cancer at age 57, and in less than two months, I will be 58. There's something quite celebratory about passing that marker in life. In my heart, I know I am still here because God has some things yet undone that He expects me to do. He has dreams for me that are bigger than I can even imagine, though I *am* dreaming big. His thoughts about me and you are above and beyond anything we could ask or think...or dream, and that's true of God's plans as well. Scripture tells us this:

God can do anything, you know—far more than you could ever imagine or guess or request in your wildest dreams! He does it not by pushing us around but by working within us, his Spirit deeply and gently within us.   (Ephesians 3:20, The Message)

Far more than our wildest dreams! And notice that it says He's not pushy. He simply works within us, gently molding and guiding our hearts and our days, like the perfect Potter that He is. And I don't know about you, but I don't want to miss a minute of His great dreams for us! I want to be fully surrendered to His plans for my life, knowing that my destiny is not about me but is about what He is going to let me do for others.

So what about you? Are you ready to surrender to His plan, knowing that whatever He plans will be greater than anything we could possibly imagine? Are you ready to wake up every day, hungry not to miss a single thing He has in store? As we walk through each day of the year, I encourage and challenge you to sing a love song to God.

I don't want to fall asleep, God, because I miss You, and I don't want to miss a thing.

Be awake, be ready, and be open to His great dreams for you. It will be a wild ride!

Making Progress

God has really had my brain in a pondering state this week, and I've been thinking about progress this morning. A few thoughts for your day . . .

One of the things I hate most is to find myself in a "same old stupid place" again. Need to lose those same 20 pounds for the umpteenth time. Need to get back in the gym. Need to, need to, need to. But then there's the other side of the coin. Today I was thinking some really positive things that God has helped me orchestrate in my life, and I could NOT have done it without Him.

First, I've been going to the gym now for just over 8 months! Last summer, I thought it might kill me, but I've made so much progress! Some days are still hard, but I'm in much better shape than I was 8 months ago. Some days, I have to pray during class: "God, I know I can do all things through You because You strengthen me," and He always gets me through. Why? Because I want to have a healthy body to serve Him longer; the health piece is about feeling good, but it's so much more about service.

Secondly, I have been eating more moderately and healthier for some time, and it's paying off. I had to make adjustments last week, but I didn't go backwards, which I often do. This morning I am thanking God for helping me learn to do everything . . . even eat . . . to His Glory!

Finally, my sweet Bible study group is no longer a dream; it's a reality, and we are in our second study! No more, "Gee, I wish I had done this," or "Wow, if I had only stuck with studying, I could be in such a different place by now." Our group has found joy and excitement in studying God's word together, and we have found fellowship! What a blessing!

So why am I sharing this today? If you find yourself in a good place, a place where you have made good progress toward being all that God desires, thank Him this morning for His mighty strength and love. But if you are where I've been so many times --- in a place of beating yourself up for letting yourself go backward --- it is NOT too late to turn things around. It is *never* too late with God. Take first steps; commit and stay the course with perseverance. Find a support group and don't quit! God gives us Christian friends to keep us accountable! And don't lose sight of this: whatever you do ---- *everything* --- do it for the glory of God! And when you do, He will bless and help you.

Learning to Say "No"

For those of you who know me personally, you will get a laugh out of this devotional. For those of you who don't, you will hear a great lesson I wish I had learned earlier: the world doesn't stop when you say "no."

All my life I have been a people pleaser and a doer. Even in my childhood and teenage years, I was involved in everything that seemed like a good idea . . . children's choir, bell choir, youth group, clubs at school, honor societies, cheerleading --- the list could go on and on. And I extended that pattern into my adult life. After child # 5, Jake, was born, I remember being PTO President at my children's elementary school, leading meetings with a baby on my hip, laundry at home that needed attention, and papers that begged to be graded for my middle school students. Yes, I was a working mom who also took on tons of extra things, mostly because I liked being involved --- it fed my spirit --- but also because I liked making people happy, a dangerous quality.

For years, my friends and family have said, "You need to learn to say 'No!'" And my come back? "I know how . . . really I do." But I didn't. You see, a lot of why I said "yes" to those things and others is that I thought I had to find my value in keeping people happy and pleased with me. I thought that I should do every-thing that came my way. Both of those ideas were misguided and not led by God.

In 2014 and 2015 an interesting thing began to happen. First, God led me to retire, something I thought I wouldn't do for a very long time. And in that retirement, I found the greatest peace and joy, and I thought to myself, "Wow, this saying 'no' is okay; the world didn't stop and I'm at peace and happier than ever before." (Quick disclaimer: I loved my years as a teacher; it was simply time, in God's plan, for me to go.) Since retirement, I've taken on a number of things and turned down a number of things, giving myself time to complete items on my retirement bucket list, but then God began to do something in my spirit: He began to move in me to let go of more things . . . to take back some time for Him and me. And in my praying about this, I found His peace about going to some folks I really love and saying, "I just can't do this for you right now." And after I did it? No earthquakes, no end-of-the-world. Just peace.

And the big shocker? They don't hate me for it, and there is someone else who will fill that gap. In fact, maybe I needed to get out of the way so someone could find purpose by filling that position. Wow. The people-pleaser has had an eye-opener.

God never intends for us to be busy; He intends for us to be fruit-ful. Now, sometimes in being fruitful and being a part of His de-sires for us, we will be busy, but as I like to say, it will be a "good busy." At night, we may be tired, but it's a "good tired" . . . a tired that comes with peace, knowing that we are walking in love and doing the things He has laid before us to do. And that kind of tired is a really satisfying thing.

I have been reading Priscilla Shirer's book *Breathe*, and she says this: "Recognition is the prerequisite of liberation." Are you enslaved to saying "yes" and don't even know it? Do you need to ask God to show you where you have forgotten to build margins into your life? Margins that give you comfort, peace, and rest?

Ask Him. He promised in Psalm 23 that we could rest beside still waters and restore our souls.

Today I will go to our farm, walk in the sunshine, and rest beside the still waters of one of the ponds. If you need to join me --- either physically or in spirit --- do this for yourself today. Allow time for rest, reflection, and a chance to breathe deeply of God's peace.

The LORD IS MY SHEPHERD, I LACK NOTHING.
He makes me lie down in green pastures,
he refreshes my soul. (Psalm 23: 1-3, HCSB)

God's Promise is Real

In South Carolina in recent weeks, we have suffered devastation the likes of which we have never seen before. Our beautiful state has been inundated with rain, and the ensuing floods have swept across cars, families, houses, and lands. As I write this, the state is still in recovery mode, and it will be quite a while before the waters completely recede. But during this time, God has done for me, and surely for others, what He promised in scripture:

"And we know that in all things God works for the good of those who love him, who have been called according to his purpose." (Romans 8:28, NIV)

Now, don't tune me out until you hear me out. No, this flood has not been good, and the suffering is real and palpable, but look at the scripture again: **in** all things, God works for the good of those who love Him. Let's settle here for just a minute, and I'll start with a story.

Two weeks ago, I was absolutely overwhelmed, and I had done it to myself. I had accepted too many responsibilities on my plate, and I felt that I was drowning. I was living from event to event, working on the next thing just hours before it happened. I admitted to a friend and my pastor that I had truly done what people always accused me of doing: saying "yes" too much. It wasn't God's fault, I did it. And, I was the one feeling like I was drowning.

The stress was showing up in my body, giving me a painful neck ache and leaving me exhausted even following a good night's sleep.

My fault . . . my problem.

But in my frustration, I called out to God. I asked Him to forgive me for accepting too much and also asked for His grace in helping me survive these few weeks until the load could lighten. You see, even in my mess, I trust Him to love me and lift me from the muck I had created. Well, He answered my prayers, but as usual, He took me by surprise in the way He answered.

We were hosting a family reunion at our new farm; it was cancelled due to the storm. I could drop those preparations and stop stressing about cleaning my house for company. I had workshops to teach, but we couldn't leave home due to the flooding, so they were postponed. I had a class to teach and material to study, but the storm gave me time to prepare myself for my students. I needed to choose music to prepare for Wednesday and Sunday, but Sunday service was cancelled and moved to Wednesday. I got everything ready and even got ahead of the game for once.

God works **IN** all things for the good of those who love Him . . . and I surely love Him.

Don't misunderstand the point: this flood has been and is terrible. Many people have suffered and I make light of nothing in this natural disaster, but I also trust God. When we give Him our tears, our fears, our hearts, and our repentance, He works **IN** all things for our good. Note that the scripture does not say that all things ARE good; it simply says that **IN** all things, He can still work for our good. After all, He is sovereign God, and He can do what looks impossible to us. My schedule truly looked impossible to my human eye, but God forgave me for accepting too much and slowed me down, providing time for me to pull myself together.

Only God could have taken such a terrible tragedy and used it for good in some small way. And He continues to do this.

Just yesterday I saw on Facebook where teens from my precious church baked cookies and delivered them to flood victims --- a small act but one that will impact them forever. They didn't just love the victims; they *acted* on their love because their leaders saw an opportunity to teach them about service and kindness in the midst of a storm.

God worked *in* that very thing for good in the hearts of teenagers.

And I've seen another thing on Facebook. People everywhere in South Carolina are devastated, and yet, over and over, they are saying things like, "God will take care of us," and "We are trusting God, no matter what happens." This is not always what we hear in the midst of tragedy, but it is becoming a beautiful testimony to the people of South Carolina who are claiming God as Sovereign and good, right there in the middle of the flood zone.

These are some of the testimonies going out about the goodness of God . . . He is working **IN** these words for good as they reach millions through Facebook and TV as well.

There's one more thing: I have heard two sermons recently that God had orchestrated way in advance of this storm. On Sunday, October 4, the church where I am blessed to serve had to cancel services due to power outages and dangerous rains. My husband

and I decided to go to a local church and worship together, and guess what the pastor had planned for his sermon way before the storms hit: the story of Noah and God's redemption. An accident? No. It was God's plan because people needed to hear this during the storm. And then on Sunday, October 11, I was able to go back to my church in Georgetown, and God did it again. Weeks before this happened, the pastor had planned a sermon series on Job . . . need I say more? Job suffered tremendously, just like people in South Carolina have been suffering, but God was there, and He delivered Job, and He will deliver us.

God went ahead of the storm, preparing what He needed His people to hear, even before the pastors and people knew they needed to hear it. Those sermons prepared our hearts to stand firm, trust God, and tell others that He is indeed good, even in the midst of disaster.

This week, our youth sticks ministry at church will share "Praise You in the Storm"; how perfect. They will remind us to continue to trust God and praise Him in the worst of our circumstances. They will remind us in a beautiful way that God really does work for good **IN** all things for those who love Him.

We need this today and every day both in South Carolina and around the world. He is good. He is good. He is good! Hallelujah!

Engraved on His Hands

Five of my children and sons-in-law have tattoos. When the first one came along, I was curious about what would cause someone to have their skin pierced with an inked needle. Really? Choosing pain? Of course, is this much different than wearing stilettos? ☺

Well, my son, Asher, explained to me that he wouldn't get just *any* tattoo, but it had to be something very significant and representative of his life and beliefs. Since that first one there have been others, and though I still don't want one for myself, there is one of his that I love. It's a beautifully scripted title of a poem that speaks his heart; he shared the poem, and it resonated with me as well. For the remainder of my teaching career, that poem lived on the wall of my classroom, and now it has a special place in my home office.

> Bullfight critics ranked in rows
>
> Crowd the enormous plaza full,
>
> But he's the only one who knows,
>
> And he's the man who fights the bull.
>
> ---Domingo Ortega

I love the poem because it reminds me that critics are often ones who don't understand what I do and yet toss their criticisms anyway. As a result of my relationship with Almighty God, I don't worry about the "critics" anymore; I live to please *Him* and Him alone, but I wasn't always this way. For a very long time, I was a people pleaser, and the critics' comments worried me, hurt me, and created doubt in me. Not anymore.

As far as the tattoo is concerned…Why did Asher choose that piece to be engraved permanently on his body? It is because it matters deeply to him . . . it speaks his heart.

Isaiah 49:16 says, "See, I have engraved you on the palms of my hands; your walls are ever before me."

In this verse, the walls being referenced are Jerusalem's walls, which are in ruins, but God says that His people are engraved on the palms of His hands. You see, He wants them to know that in their devastation and destruction, He has not forgotten them. In fact, He loves them deeply and completely.

God engraves us on His palms because we are the thing that matters to Him most. He sees our hurt, our destruction, our devastation, and our sadness, and He has not left us. He couldn't; He loves us too much.

In recent years and after much "growing up" in God, I have finally come to the end of needing to please the critics. I have recently given myself permission, after much prayer, to drop out of some things that please others but quite honestly don't please me nor fit into God's plan for me. And do you know what? I'm sure the critics are out there, but it simply doesn't matter anymore. I rise every morning to please God, my Father, and I put my head on the pillow at night, satisfied to seek Him and only Him. Are the bullfight critics still out there, ranked in rows, waiting to tear me and others down? Oh, yes, they are always waiting, but here's what I know: when we give ourselves over to God, the people in the plaza have no power over us, and in fact, they can become ones for whom we pray regularly. The haters can continue to hate, but they cannot continue to hurt when we choose to love them, pray for them, and not let their opinions decide for us what only God can decide.

I'm An Addict

Hello. My name is Jean Burden, and I am a food addict.

I've avoided saying this for years for a number of reasons. First, I remember that quite a few years ago. In my Sunday school class I mentioned serious overeating as a sin. I was laughed out of the class, and clearly, the other folks in the room thought the problem of eating was a Southern thing . . . a joke . . . *definitely not* a sin.

I have also avoided saying it because I refused to recognize it as an addiction until recently. Until a few years ago, I was able to cut back, go the gym, walk, and keep my weight in check. But two things have left me undone: menopause and a loss of eating control.

My name is Jean Burden, and I am a food addict.

So how did I figure this out? I began to pray and pay attention, and I noticed some unhealthy things about myself. When others snacked slowly in a meeting, I snacked nonstop. When others didn't go back for seconds, I always did. When I said I wouldn't eat the sweets, I did it anyway. And worse? One piece of pound cake was never enough. When I prayed, God revealed things to me that were pretty ugly.

My name is Jean Burden, and I am a food addict. And in the

words of Priscilla Shirer in her book *Breathe*, "I must recognize this slavery to fix it."[1]

I'm not joining Eaters Anonymous, if there is such a thing, and right now I'm not returning to Weight Watchers, though it is an excellent program. I am giving this thorn in my side to God, knowing that He will give me the strength and power from His Word and His Hand to deal with this addiction. And He can do this for you, too . . . whatever your addiction might be.

In 1 Corinthians 10:13, we find this, "No temptation has overtaken you except what is common to humanity." God is faithful, and He will not allow you to be tempted beyond what you are able but with the temptation He will also provide a way of escape so that you are able to bear it.

And so we can learn a few things here. First, any temptation we have is not new, and we are not the only ones dealing with it. Our temptations are common to humanity, and though I am sad that others are fighting this food battle, it's nice to know that it's not just me. Second, God is faithful. In my own strength, I may fall apart and eat the cheesecake, but God is faithful even when I am weak. Third, and probably most important: He always provides a way out, an escape, so we can bear the temptation without falling into sin. Wow. Since pondering this, I have been looking for His way out. When I am tempted to do what's bad for me and my body **– His holy temple –** I pay attention to Godly escape routes.

Now another thing to know: Satan will not hit us with temptation once and give up. He will come again and again and again because he needs us to fail. But Jesus is our model.

When Jesus went into the wilderness and was tempted by Satan, it wasn't just once, and yet every time, Jesus came back at him with God's Word. He trusted His Father to be faithful and he told Satan to go away. I know I can do these things as well. And there's something else I can do: phone a friend.

Just yesterday I called a friend who is being successful in her weight control right now, but like me, she has struggled. I called her because I have been watching her success, and I knew she could be a great support and advisor to me. Sometimes we need to phone a friend, and I think that's okay with God. First we go to Him, and then we find a Christian sister or brother who can stand with us in the battle. It's always good to stand firm together.

For those of you who have not fought this particular fight and are still not convinced that this is an issue, let me share one final thing. Anything we do that gets in the way of serving God becomes an idol and a sin. My eating has become an idol, and any idol is a serious problem. I want to serve God all my days, speaking and singing and going places for Him, and I can't do that if my body is not in its best possible condition. I can't look others in the eye and tell them to seek God to control their addictions, whether they are food, drugs, sex, pornography . . . *whatever* they may be . . . if I won't or can't control my own.

Yes, I am a food addict, and it has taught me humility.

"Father, forgive me for the times in my life when I have been judgmental in my spirit about others who can't control their addictions. Never let me forget this powerful lesson."

Maybe you are like me. You have stood in judgment because you haven't walked in an addict's shoes. Be careful: God will allow a thorn in your side if it means He can teach you a lesson about loving others, empathizing with them, and becoming humble in order to serve Him fully.

Search your own heart today, and if, like me, you need His forgiveness, simply ask for it. Humble yourselves before Almighty, Sovereign God, and let Him create a right spirit within you: a spirit of love, humility, and self-control. He is waiting to transform your heart into a healthy one, both physically and spiritually, and this gives me joy.

Hello. My name is Jean Burden, and I am a food addict. But God is in control, and with Him, all things are possible.

1 Corinthians 10:13, "No temptation has overtaken you except what is common to mankind. And God is faithful; he will not let you be tempted beyond what you can bear. But when you are tempted, he will also provide a way out so that you can endure it." (NIV)

Mark 10:27, "Jesus looked at them and said, "With man this is impossible, but not with God; all things are possible with God." (NIV)

Strengthening Our Cores

In the summer of 2015, I began attending yoga classes at our local recreation center. The practices were very hard for me at first because I was terribly out of shape, but over time, my body has become way more flexible and my muscles are getting stronger. I love the quietness of the yoga room, and I find myself lifting words to God throughout the class, sometimes asking Him to give me strength I don't have! One of the weakest places in my body seems to be my core, and in yoga the instructor is constantly saying, "Don't forget to keep your core tight." With each class I'm getting better, one practice at a time, but every time she mentions the core, I think about our spiritual practices. We need a strong core as well.

In Ephesians, Paul writes about putting on the full armor of God, and one of the first pieces of armor is the belt, or girdle, of truth. Roman soldiers put on the girdle first to stabilize and strengthen the core of the body, and we must do the same. Every day we need to be learning something from God's Word about His Truth for our lives. We need to be girding ourselves --- our cores ---- with His Words so in times of joy or times of trial we can stand up against Satan and the storms of life with a core that is girded with God's promises. But we can't do that if we aren't immersing ourselves in those very words, placing them in our minds, our mouths, and our hearts so we are ready for battle.

Recently I've been leading a Priscilla Shirer study, *Armor of God*, and during the week in which we studied the section on keeping our peace, you know that Satan came after us to do his worst. I found my peace being attacked at every turn by circumstances at home and even at church. But, I fought back. What was my weapon of choice? God's very words about how to keep my peace. You see, I have been strengthening my core with scriptures about peace, and so I was ready for the attack. I prayed God's Words back to Him: "Jesus, you promised us peace, not as the world understands it, but Your peace, and I am claiming that right now." And because my attack happened to be about other people who I was allowing to frustrate me, I also prayed, "God, You told me in Your Word that Your compassions fail not every morning, and I need You to keep my heart humble and compassionate as well." Through these simple prayers, my peace returned, but it would not have happened had I not been keeping my core wrapped in God's Word and prayer.

And there's another yoga lesson I want to share. Many times we are told to keep certain parts of the body tight but other parts completely relaxed. An example might be to keep the core and legs tight during a particular pose but relax the shoulders, keeping them down and at rest. Interesting idea, and I know there's a spiritual principle here as well. If we keep our core strong with God's Word and prayer, we should be able to relax into our journey here on earth. We should be able to enjoy every day, even in the midst of trials and tribulations, because God is in charge. He is with us every step of the way, giving us strength when we are weak and holding our tears in His mighty hands. Isn't that a wonderful picture? We can relax into His arms and fall at the feet of our Savior, resting in His presence, which brings me to one more lesson.

In yoga we are always told that when we need to rest a minute, especially if a pose becomes too much for us, we are to move into "child's pose." This is a resting place with our faces down on the floor and our arms stretched out beyond our heads. (You know where I'm going with this!) When life gets to be too much and we feel we can't go on, we desperately need to get into "child's pose" at the throne of God, our Father. We need to rest with our faces bowed in humility and gratitude, knowing that He has told us to rest beside His still waters to restore our strength. We need to curl up before our Savior and be like little children, trusting Him to comfort, revive, and renew. We need to breathe deeply, in and out, breathing in His Spirit, His presence, and His love. And just like in yoga, when we have regained our strength and our peace, we can move back into the tougher poses of life, ready to be strong in our cores while relaxing into whatever the day brings.

I will continue to practice yoga in the coming days and years because it keeps me healthier and stronger. I often have tension in my neck, and I always find relief in class. I am grateful to have found this wonderful practice at this time in my life, and I always ask God to help me so I can be physically strong to serve Him as long as He will use me. And I want the same for my spiritual core. I want to keep girding myself with His Truth so I can meet every circumstance with peace, standing up tall and strong, always ready to serve Him everywhere I go.

I encourage you to find scriptures that you can pray back to God. Commit them to your heart and be strong in the Lord by always standing tall with a tight core, girded by His Word, and going into "child's pose" when you need to rest before your Father. Just like yoga has become for me, let this be a daily practice for you so you can truly enjoy this journey on earth. We don't have to wait for heaven to be strong and at peace . . . with a tight core of God's Truth, we can have it right now, right here on earth.

At the end of class, we always place prayer hands in front of our hearts and say the word *namaste*. I looked it up and this is what I found:

"The gesture Namaste represents the belief that there is a Divine spark within each of us that is located in the heart chakra. The gesture is an acknowledgment of the soul in one by the soul in another. *Nama* means bow, *as* means I, and *te* means you. Therefore, *namaste* literally means "bow me you" or "I bow to you."

How perfect. You have God within you in the form of the Holy Spirit, and so I close this devotional with prayer hands in front of my heart, thinking of you and knowing that I bow to God, grateful that He lives within you and me. I am grateful also that our mutual trust in God makes us brothers and sisters in Christ. Amen and Amen.

***I don't usually do this but this devotional is dedicated first to God, but also to Charlean and Ashley, my yoga instructors at the Conway Recreation Center. Thank you for being patient teachers as I am learning to be strong.

10-12 And that about wraps it up. God is strong, and he wants you strong. So take everything the Master has set out for you, well-made weapons of the best materials. And put them to use so you will be able to stand up to everything the Devil throws your way. This is no afternoon athletic contest that we'll walk away from and forget about in a couple of hours. This is for keeps, a life-or-death fight to the finish against the Devil and all his angels.

13-18 Be prepared. You're up against far more than you can handle on your own. Take all the help you can get, every weapon God has issued, so that when it's all over but the shouting you'll still be on your feet. Truth, righteousness, peace, faith, and salvation are more than words. Learn how to apply them. You'll need them throughout your life. God's Word is an *indispensable* weapon. In the same way, prayer is essential in this ongoing warfare. Pray hard and long. Pray for your brothers and sisters. Keep your eyes open. Keep each other's spirits up so that no one falls behind or drops out.   (Ephesians 6:10-18, The Message)

http://www.yogajournal.com/article/beginners/the-meaning-of-quot-namaste-quot/

The Dividing Wall

I have spent the last 36 years of my life as a teacher in one capacity or another. For 34 years, I taught in public schools in South Carolina, and for the past two years, I have been serving students at the college level and as a teacher-recruiter in high schools. I love and value young people. God allowed me . . . even pushed me . . . to walk in my calling as one who would value them enough to work with them daily and be a role model for their lives. He called me there for a number of reasons, but I believe one reason is that He gave me the ability to love *ALL* children ---- children of all personalities, all races, all backgrounds, and all abilities. Loving them, forgiving them when necessary, and guiding them all came easy because God enabled me. The world doesn't seem to be doing so well in this capacity and quite frankly, I am distressed and afraid of where we are headed.

All over our country people of different races are distrusting each other, sometimes for what seems, on the surface, to be very good reasons. Young people are losing their lives, and every shot and motive is under a microscope. People are questioning every move of celebrities who encourage racial pride. This is not the world God wants for us and surely not the world I can accept for myself.

From early in history, groups have distrusted and been antagonistic toward each other. But God says this simply doesn't have to be the way we live. In Priscilla Shirer's study, *Armor of God*, she states: "Are hurt and anger lingering between you and another person? . . . Between one race and another? The peace of God can bridge the gap to bring healing and restoration. And when it does, not only will it cause the people around here on this planet to sit up and notice, but it will declare the manifold wisdom of God through the church 'to the rulers and authorities in the heavens' (Ephesians 3: 10). In other words, unity among once-divided brothers and sisters puts Satan promptly in his place." [1]

"For He is our peace, who made both groups one and tore down the dividing wall of hostility." (Ephesians 2:14)

So, why are still having problems?

I just don't believe we are believing God for what He promised us. If we *really* believed Him, we would seek peace above discord, we would look for ways to bring peace to every situation, and we would go the extra mile to create peace in our churches, our communities, and our nation.

And, I don't care what we think the other person or group has done. It is our responsibility as Christians...**Christ-followers**...to love in response to EVERYTHING! (**Can you hear my voice**?)

EVERYTHING! We are to pray for people who feel like our enemies, and when we do that, it is almost impossible to hate. We are to ask God to bless others whom we don't understand, and when we do that, God can move in *OUR* hearts, softening us to His kind of complete compassion. When we ask Him to help us see people and the world with "Jesus-glasses," He will change our vision, and we will realize that much of what steals our peace could be changed with listening ears and a compassionate heart.

But this can only be achieved with God's kind of peace, the peace the world doesn't understand. The peace that passes human understanding. In other words, we need the kind of miracle peace that Jesus promised, and we can have it.

Just this week I happened to see a Dr. Phil show about feuding neighbors. He never really got to the bottom of truth, but it was clear that there were serious issues of hatred, judgment, and antagonism going on. Dr. Phil finally asked both families to put the past in the past and hit the reset button, making choices from that moment on to look for ways to be healers, not harmers, in their neighborhood. They all agreed, but I'm not sure it will happen. Surprising attitude from me, the eternal optimist, right? Well, here's what I know. Dr. Phil gave them good advice, but what he didn't say it this: God is the only one who can give us all a heart transplant, carving out the fear and hatred and replacing it with forgiveness, acceptance, and love. Unless these families find it in themselves to give their hearts to Christ, I don't think this will ever be solved in the way it could be, if only God would be allowed in the situation. Which brings me to another point . . .

We can continue as a people and a nation to hate and fight and distrust. We don't have to give our hearts and our nation to God, and as long as we behave like we don't want him in our lives and our country, I can promise you that He will stay out of our messes, allowing us to continue on this destructive path. We can go to every prayer meeting and Bible study, but if we don't allow God to work in us in a personal way, removing the wrong things from our hearts and letting him develop in us the fruits of the Spirit, then nothing will change. People who claim Christ will continue to post ugly things on Facebook about people they don't like, and people who don't claim Christ will continue to see validation in the division.

It is time for all of us to do a few urgent things: 1) We need to ask the Holy Spirit to guide our hearts, our words, and our minds to love. Yes, love. Jesus gave us that beautiful command . . . to love one another. Not just the people we WANT to love, but ALL people. 2) We need to go on a word fast, eliminating anything that hints of judgment, hatred, and division, especially in social media. If you are tempted to say something horrible on Facebook about anyone, ask yourself this: would Christ be pleased? And who would this statement help? 3) We need to pray fervently for those we love the least. Once again in the words of Priscilla Shirer, "...unity among once-divided brothers and sisters puts Satan promptly in his place." [2]

Ephesians 2:14 tells us this, "For He is our peace, who made both groups one and tore down the dividing wall of hostility." (HCSB) God doesn't just want peace; He IS peace, and He has torn down any wall of hostility that Satan has tried to erect. We are the only ones who can build that dividing wall again with our attitudes and our lack of love. And when we allow Satan to build walls in our hearts, we lose our peace, the very peace that Christ promised us.

So this year, give up hatred. Give up negative words toward and about others. Give up the dividing wall. Let God give you peace with Him, peace with others, and peace in your own heart. Be an agent of peace and love and harmony in your home, your church, your community, and your nation. In the words of a very favorite song of mine, "Let it be said of us, we were marked be forgiveness; we were known by our love and delighted in meekness. We were ruled by our grace, heeding unity's call. Joined as one body, that Christ would be seen by all."

Let it be said of us.

Only God

I am an extrovert to the 10th power. I love being with people, and according to the true definition of an extrovert, I gain energy when I am in a crowd. When I was in a middle school classroom, it didn't matter how tired or achy I was when I got to school; I always found my stride and energy from being with those adolescent, hormonal children! So here's something interesting.

I also love being alone and love being quiet. *Love* it. Just this morning, I locked the doors of my house after my husband left, lit a candle, and turned off all the noise. Then I went to the couch to sit, pray, and be alone. Not lonely. Just alone. Years ago I didn't know what to do with "alone" time, but now I do. God has taken this total extrovert and transformed a part of me into one who cherishes a quiet house, a peaceful walk at our farm (Boggy Road Palm and Lily Farm), and time with just Him and me. It took a lot of patience on His part to bring me to this place. I had spent so many years being surrounded by my children, my husband, my students, and my church family, that when down time came, I felt insecure and lonely. I simply didn't know how to appreciate being in a quiet place without distractions, without people, without noise. But now I do.

God is really amazing

Only God could take an extrovert like me and change me into a person who seeks quiet spaces in order to seek Him. Only God could take introverted women I have known and give them urgent things to say for His kingdom, enabling them to have the courage and the words. Only God could take the messes I and others have made and turn them into blessings and messages for others to hear. Only God could take an abused young woman and turn her into a pastor with a powerful heart that hungers to love Him and serve His people. Only God could take people like me who have committed so many sins, cleansing us with the blood of Jesus, and allowing us to serve Him in His kingdom.

Only God

I watch commercials almost every day that promise change. They promise weight loss and better bodies. They promise the power to quit smoking and the power to change a future. But here's the truth that I have found: none of those things work in my human power. They only work when God is behind and in the middle of the change. He is a transforming God, who delights in drawing us to Him, that we might become closer and closer to what He desires for us. And what is that? To be like Christ.

To be like Christ. A tall order? Yes. A lofty goal? Yes. But here's the thing: it is not a destination; it is a journey and one to be enjoyed and celebrated. With every day that we allow God to own and inhabit every place of our beings . . . every inch of our hearts and souls . . . He is able to change our thinking, our loving, our habits, and our minds. But we must take the first step. We must surrender. Everything. Anything we hold back will hold us back because God will only work in the places we give to Him, the places we trust to His mighty hands, the places we are scared to death to surrender. But surrender we must, and when we do, we don't find slavery . . . we find freedom. Complete freedom!

Doe on the Run

This week I witnessed something I have never seen before. It captured both my attention and my heart. I had walked onto my new back porch to look at a flock of geese that had landed in our big pond, and while I was preparing to take a picture, I heard a splash . . . a *big* splash. My eyes scrambled for the cause, and I saw a deer in the water! She was swimming as quickly as possible, and I soon knew why: there were two dogs after her. Dan and I watched her and the chase until she seemed to slip away from them, into the safety of our woods. The whole thing bothered me greatly, which is odd since I grew up with and am married to a hunter. (No one in my family ever hunted with dogs.) Something about watching it disturbed my spirit, and I found myself cheering for her to get away. I even secretly wished that Dan could stop those dogs somehow.

I wanted to shout, "This is private property! Go away!" Silly, I know, but I wanted the chase to end, knowing that if they caught her, it would be sure death.

Okay, so this morning, I gazed at the pond and replayed the scene in my brain. And here's what God nudged into my spirit: just like that beautiful doe, we will always be under attack by evil that seeks to "steal, kill, and destroy." And just like that doe, we will always have cheerleaders on the sidelines, encouraging us to escape and have victory. So let's break this down a little.

First of all, in John 10: 10, we read this: "The thief comes only to steal and kill and destroy. I have come so they can have life. I want them to have it in the fullest possible way." To continue our analogy, those dogs were there to do one thing: track that deer so their owner could kill and destroy. (Disclaimer: I'm not knocking deer hunters, in fact, I love venison. Just go with the analogy!) Satan does the exact same thing in our lives. He sends "dogs" after us, to track us, to drag us down, and prepare us to be destroyed. The "dogs" are things like discouragement, anger, frustration, and temptation to sin, and there are more...lust, greed, envy, gossip...the list is endless. Satan knows precisely the very thing that gets us, and he sends that very thing our way that has the greatest potential for taking us down. He is a thief, and his only goal is to destroy our worship and our witness, leaving us hopeless, defeated, and separated from God.

The second part of the verse says that Jesus came that we might have life; in fact, He says that we can have a full life! Another scripture says that God will always provide a way out, if we but seek Him and ask. The doe found a way out: she swam as fast as she could away from those dogs, and then she disappeared into the woods just beyond the water. God has "woods" waiting for us, too. In Nahum (not our everyday reading!) it says, "The LORD is good, a stronghold in the day of trouble; and He knows those who trust in Him." A stronghold . . . safe woods. He promises that this is available to us. In 2 Corinthians 4: 8-9, we are given another promise, "We are hard-pressed on every side, yet not crushed; we are perplexed, but not in despair; persecuted, but not forsaken; struck down, but not destroyed." Think about it: the thief, Satan, comes to destroy, but God says we may be perplexed, in despair, and persecuted, and yet, we are **NOT** destroyed. Victory...we simply *don't* have to give in to loss.

And finally, remember that I was on the porch, cheering for the doe? Well, God says we have cheerleaders, so to speak. In Hebrews 12: 1, we are told that we are surrounded by "a great cloud of witnesses." I like to imagine this scene: we are running in a great stadium, on a track, and the race is long and arduous. In the stands, cheering us on, we see Moses, Abraham, Joseph, Mary, David . . . the list goes on and on. These are the saints who have faithfully gone before us, and they are cheering for us as we run the race God has given us to complete. Maybe they see us almost drowning in the pond, swimming for our lives, and they are cheering to remind us that we *can* run this race of life with perseverance and victory. They did, and they are no different than we are. **They were ordinary people who followed and trusted an extraordinary God.**

Are they the only cheerleaders? No. I can see my mother, my grandmothers, and some dear friends who have finished their races, and they are cheering alongside Paul, and Peter, and Mary Magdalene, praying for us to reach the safety of God's protection. Today, I will sing praises to a God who gives me safety when I am in danger. Today, I will praise Him who promises and never fails to do what He says He will do. Today, I will remember that others have had victories against Satan and have gone on to be with God. Today, I will remember the doe and know that when I am under attack by Satan, I *always* have a way out. With God, we never have to be destroyed or in despair. And all God's people said, "Amen!"

Harper and the Cross

Recently, I went to my daughter's house to give her a ride to a ballgame. As soon as I walked into the house, I heard, "Grandma, I see da cross!" Now, I know what that means. Harper, my granddaughter, is amazed with the big cross that hangs in the sanctuary at Herbert Memorial United Methodist Church. The first time she saw it, she couldn't be quiet in church because she kept talking about it. She said, "That's a big cross, Grandma!"

This past Sunday, she was having a rough morning, and I took her to the sanctuary to settle her for a few minutes, and immediately she said it again, "There's da big cross, Grandma!" I told her that we keep the cross close to remind us always about Jesus and His sacrifice for us, and she then proceeded to find little crosses around the sanctuary . . . on top of the Christian flag, on the door . . . searching for crosses.

And you know there's a lesson here. When I went to her house last night, that cross was still on her mind, and she wanted to see it. How many of us keep the Cross on our minds so much that we hunger to see it? When I asked Harper to tell her Mommy and Daddy what the Cross reminds us of, she quickly said, "Jesus!"

How many of us constantly think about the Cross, letting it remind us daily of Jesus and His incredible sacrifice for our sinful lives?

Harper and Lily love going to church with me. Yesterday, Harper asked me if it was time to go back. I responded, "No, baby, but I promise you that Sunday is coming." Let's ask ourselves: are we as excited as she is about worship that on Monday we are already anticipating next Sunday, anxious to be in God's house and see the Cross? Do we prepare our hearts to sing with passion at every service, allowing the Holy Spirit to move through music as we worship our Father?

Jesus talked about our coming to Him as little children, and I love that image. Let us all run to Him in complete trust and passion, and like Harper, wake up daily to seek the Cross and another chance to worship. Like Harper, let us not be afraid to squeal with delight and awe when we are in the presence of our Savior, and let us --- yes, like Harper, again --- always be hungry for our next encounter with all that reminds us of who we are in Christ.

Thank you, God, for lessons learned from the children.

Saving One More

This morning in the quiet of the early day, I flipped the channels and found Schindler's List, not exactly a Hallmark Christmas movie, and yet I sat and watched. It's been many years since I first watched this film, and it moved me more today than when I first watched it in 1993. If you are too young to know his story, Oskar Schindler was a war profiteer who used his flair, his money, and his bribery to save over 1,000 Jews from death during the Nazi Holocaust. He did this at the risk of his own life, and his grand gestures and humanitarian efforts left him penniless. He lost everything but saved a generation of Jews. Just after the war ended and Schindler was fleeing to save his own life, this conversation occurred:

Oskar Schindler: I could have got more, I could have got more. I don't know. If I just...I could have got more.

Itzhak Stern: Oskar, there are 1,100 people who are alive because of you, look at them.

Oskar Schindler: If I had made more money. I threw away so much money. (laughs...then, gets teary eyed) You have no idea. if I just...

Itzhak Stern: There will be generations because of you.

Oskar Schindler: I didn't do enough.

Itzhak Stern: You did so much.

Oskar Schindler: This car. Goeth would have bought this car. Why did I keep the car? Ten people right there. Ten people. Ten more people. This pin...two people. This is gold. Two people. He would have given me two more, at least one. One more person, a person, Stern, for this. (starts crying) I could have got one more person, and I didn't! I -- I -- I -- I didn't!

End Scene.

I sobbed as a watched. One more . . . two more . . . he saved so many and yet felt he didn't do enough. I sobbed because the story is real and it is beyond heartbreaking comprehension.

I sobbed because I spend every day not doing enough.

As Christians, we know what it means to be saved. We live every day by God's grace and with His love and forgiveness, and yet what am I *doing* in this season of life? Singing one more song? Leading one more service for those who already know the saving power of Jesus? Buying one more ridiculously expensive toy? Or filling my cabinets and closets with more than I can use?

What am I doing?

Every day people leave this earth, not saved from sure destruction. Every day, people struggle with addiction and poverty and emptiness. Every day we have the power to do more. To save one more. To stop throwing away our resources and use them for good. Every day we have the power to choose.

I cry this morning because I look at my life and can't help but ask: what would God have me do today that would change one life, because as Itshak Stern says in the movie, "Whoever saves one life saves the entire world."

I am 57 years old and I don't want to be leaving this earth with a heart full of wishes . . . wishes that I had done more, wishes that I had shared more, wishes that I had wasted less and made more of a difference. Wishes are worthless without action. Today, I challenge myself first and then all of us to stop wishing and start doing. We don't have to create something new. God is already working all around us, and we simply must ask how we can be privileged to be a part of His grand plan to save the world. Jesus came as a baby, and we celebrate Christmas to celebrate His birth. But the reason He came was to save the world, and He is never satisfied until *every single one* is saved. Let us be more like Him today. Let us never rest until every single one knows the power and truth of the living Savior.

Satan and My Past

In my studying recently, I read about Satan's strategies for derailing God's plans for me. Priscilla Shirer writes this in her book "Fervent", "...that's the enemy's way. Precision, personalization, and persistence."[1] Yes, the enemy knows each one of us personally and knows exactly what to use against us to derail our prayers and our closeness to God.

And he knows me. He knows that one of the ways he can distract me and steal power is to remind me of my past failures, particularly with my children. And until yesterday, when I was praying in my car for my children and grandchildren, I didn't recognize this strategy as coming from Satan. But all of a sudden, when a reminder of something from years ago entered my mind as I prayed for my family, I realized in a flash that it was Satan's precision and personalization. He knew exactly what to do to make me doubt that my prayers for my children would be answered.

Well, I've got his number now. I know his strategy and recognize that it is his attempt to make me a doubter instead of a believer. Now that I know, I won't let him use this against me again.

So why am I sharing this? God nudged me to share because we ALL must recognize Satan's attacks on us so we are always ready to defend against them with God's armor. And *our* armor? Truth from His Word, fervent prayer, and seeking minute by minute to live out this life of righteousness He, our Father, has given us through His only Son.

In the midst of this revelation, God also nudged me with an acronym, so I want to share, just in case it can help you as well. It is my reminder that Satan doesn't get to use anything from my past against me because God has forgiven and redeemed every single moment.

P = perpetuate. I will not allow Satan to perpetuate my past or make me feel guilty about it ever again.

A = advance. I will not allow Satan to advance anything negative from my past into my present or future.

S = stay. I will not allow guilt or Satan to stay in the room of my heart.

T = talk about it. I will not talk about my past mistakes because reliving them over and over in conversation gives them life and power that they no longer have.

PAST: if you have not asked God to forgive you of something and Satan is trying to use it against you, go straight to the Father today. Let Him make your heart "white as snow." And then? Let it go.

And if you have already asked God's forgiveness for anything, don't let Satan bring it back to you again and again. He simply wants to destroy your confidence in God's ability to forgive and give us a hope and a future free of condemnation and guilt.

I leave you with these words from Priscilla Shirer, "God calls you to purity because He wants your hearts protected and at rest, inhospitable to the devil and his intentions. God wants you full of power and confidence and spiritual vitality. He wants you free to bless and encourage others, to receive and celebrate His goodness, to become such a stick-of-dynamite prayer warrior that Satan just hates hearing your coffeepot heat up in the morning." [2]

My coffeepot is hot and my heart is at peace. I pray that yours is as well.

Blessings!

Empty to Full

Empty. This word carries positive feelings, negative connotations, and even neutral messages. When my laundry hamper is empty, I'm relieved to be finished with a task. When my wallet is empty, I know I must be careful with my spending. When my coffee cup is empty, I refill . . . and quickly!

Empty. But there are serious implications to emptiness, too.

Politics . . . often full of empty promises that sound convincing but are never fulfilled.

Poverty . . . empty pantries and families who don't have enough to eat.

Infertility . . . couples with empty hearts, hungering to parent a child with unconditional love.

Hearts . . . starving for something and looking in the wrong places to be filled.

Emptiness.

But then there's Jesus.

Recently I bought a set of "Resurrection Eggs" for my grandchildren, hoping they would begin to understand the pieces of the Easter story. In every egg there is a symbol of the story . . . a donkey, a rooster, a whip, nails . . . and then there's the last egg: it's empty! My granddaughters love to open the last one and squeal with delight, knowing that the empty, white egg means that Jesus isn't in the tomb anymore. The tomb is empty because He's alive! They know how it ends but still have the same excitement every single time we go through that box of Resurrection Eggs --- excitement for the emptiness of the tomb.

So what else is empty that we can celebrate? And what does God do with our emptiness? Let's take a look for a moment.

In the Old Testament, the Israelites wandered in the wilderness for forty years, and during that time, their empty stomachs were filled by God's great provision. He provided manna every day to sustain His people. In the New Testament, people's stomachs were empty once again. It was after Jesus had been teaching to thousands, and they were hungry. Jesus took five loaves and two fishes from a young boy who gave it all to Him, and when the day was over, everyone was full, and there was much food left over. Jesus performed a miracle of the blessing and the breaking of the bread, and the emptiness was remedied.

In Psalm 23, probably the most familiar Psalm in the Bible, God promises that we do not have to want for anything. "The Lord is my Shepherd; I shall not want." No emptiness here. And in the New Testament (in Acts) the followers of Jesus felt empty and alone because He had returned to heaven, but God sent the Holy Spirit to fill them completely. No emptiness for believers.

And then there's the Cross. Our Savior is not there. He does not reside on the Cross because His time there was temporary. He chose to die there for us but not to stay there. And He didn't stay in the tomb either. His burial clothes were left in the tomb

. . . empty. And in case you're not sure, He was **not** stolen; He arose and walked away from the tomb, fulfilling all prophecy ever written about Him.

Empty clothes, an empty cross, and an empty tomb. Emptiness that is a cause for celebration!

Today and every day we need to follow the example of my granddaughters: we need to squeal with delight because the empty tomb means Jesus did exactly what He said He would do: He arose and went to heaven to sit on the Mercy Seat for us. He sits there today, waiting on us to bow before Him, bringing Him our empty hearts or our full hearts. It matters not. He accepts us as we are. And as He told the Samaritan woman at the well, He will fill us with living water so we will never thirst again!

The Joy of Gardening

I don't know of any hobby I love more than gardening. The passion for it is embedded deep in my soul, going way back to my Mama Belle. I used to walk in her backyard, amazed at the impatiens blooming everywhere, and that was just one plant. She had so many, and she knew each one by name, and what's more . . . she knew the care each one needed. My father was the same way, and I am humbly and happily following in their footsteps.

We moved into a new home in October 2015, but the summer of 2015 was all about creating new homes for my plants and establishing a new "hospital" for the ones that were suffering. As soon as we had our first Southern, warm, late winter day, I began checking on my hospital to see what might be happening. I also added a new feature: intensive care --- AKA a baby swimming pool with water in it. The very driest, worst looking plants went into intensive care, and there they have stayed. But here's the excitement: today was moving day! Plants left the hospital, and the ones in intensive care have new growth! It may sound silly to those of you who don't love playing in the dirt, but to me, there couldn't be better news. My love and care have paid off, and I have beautiful flowers to enjoy in the months ahead. And enjoy I will!

Plants and flowers bring a certain peace to the spirit. They are quiet, sometimes unassuming and other times quite showy, and they respond to love and pampering. They grow with the right fertilizer and light, and they die back in season. To everything there is a season . . .

We could learn a lot from plants about how to treat people in the world.

Before Jesus left us to be with His Father, He gave us a last-minute command: Love one another. In the HCSB, John 13:34 sounds like this: "I give you a new command: Love one another. Just as I have loved you, you must also love one another."

And this is not the only time He commanded us to love. In Matthew, He told us to love our enemies and pray for those who persecute us. And in other places in John, we read it again: our **command** . . . not our request . . . is to love one another. Obviously this was huge. Jesus said it more than once, He said it just before He left to go back to Heaven, and he required it of us. So what does this love look like?

Well, sometimes it looks like my plants that need to be in the hospital. Sometimes we see people who look scraggly and hopeless, no longer growing and producing anything at all. Jesus didn't say to love just the showy ones; He said to love . . . period. So sometimes we have to love with lots of action. Love is a verb, remember? We have to take time with people, give them extra care, and check on them daily. These are not always the folks who respond quickly to our love either. They can take a very long time and yet we don't read anywhere that God told us to give up on love. And so we love and love and love some more. And then there's intensive care.

Sometimes things are so bleak in this world that people have simply quit. Their spirits are empty and are desperate to be filled. I want to tell you a story about Hannah, our sweet granddaughter. Hannah seems to have a very perceptive spirit about people, and just recently, her perception showed up in love and paid big dividends. She was in church, and as children often do, she got up to go to the restroom. The only thing is this: Hannah doesn't usually do that, so God surely had an appointment for her. As she walked toward the bathrooms, she felt the need to reach out a hug a lady in her seat, telling this woman that she loved her. Only God could have known that this woman was in a deep place of discouragement, overloaded with life-junk that was weighing her down into a very dark place. But then came Hannah's honest, simple, and pure love. And what was this woman's response? She called Hannah's mom and shared: that very moment healed her spirit. **Healed her.** Did you hear that? Just an act of love from someone doing exactly what God placed her on that aisle to do.

Intensive care? Yes. Healing possible? Oh, yes. Our God is the God of the impossible broken heart, the impossible situation, and the impossible emptiness. He used a child and He is preparing appointments for you and me to be used to love people in our path. Sometimes it will be as simple as a hug and a word, and at other times, it will require much more of us, but God-appointments cannot be ignored because someone out there needs us to be an answer to prayer, and we need the blessing that comes from obeying God with love.

And one last thing: love can't be contained in church. There are people right within the walls of our churches who desperately need our love, and we need to keep our eyes open and our hearts ready. But there are millions outside those walls who are hurting in ways we cannot even imagine, and they need our love, too. It's the ultimate fertilizer and healing agent in a broken world.

So, slow down and watch for where God needs you to love. Be the Samaritan on the road who took time, energy and money to help someone who didn't look like him. Be kind and patient with angry people in line in Wal-Mart. Be intentional with your love. God surely is. When we wake up every day, He has spent His night watching over us in love, like the perfect Father He is, and His love goes with us everywhere we go. Let that be true of us, His children as well. Dionne Warwick sang it best years ago . . . "What the world needs now is love sweet love. It's the only thing that there's just too little of." Infuse your world today with love and watch those "plants" perk up in ways you never imagined!

A Beautiful Inheritance

My choice is you, GOD, first and only.
And now I find I'm *your* choice!
You set me up with a house and yard.
And then you made me your heir!

<u>The Message</u> **(MSG)   Psalm 16: 5-6**

One year ago, my husband and I broke ground on a new home. It was an incredibly exciting time, and I walked the property many days during construction, praying prayers of thanksgiving. As the contractors worked in the suffocating heat, I worked, too. I began moving my cherished plants and flowers from my old house to the new location. I used existing chunks of multi-colored granite to create shaded flower beds, and over time, I filled the beds with my own greenery. I also created a "plant hospital," moving my planters from the old deck to this shaded spot. I watered, babied, and protected everything, and even plants that looked dead and hopeless began to sprout forth new life this spring. My heart has soared with joy as I've watched it happen, and now as I walk around, I see growth everywhere! The plants are healthier than ever before, and flowers that used to struggle are blooming with vibrant color and a renewed sense of life. Just yesterday I found amaryllis blooming that had never done well before, and even in my indoor sunroom, African violets are thriving when I have never had any luck with them in the past. Yes, I have watered and fertilized, but there's another truth I know for sure: everything is reaching its fullest potential because we are in a perfect location and every plant is being given its greatest chance to show off because of the perfect combination of sunlight, shade, soil, and care.

Where my plants and flowers are concerned, this precious land is a beautiful inheritance, and it's true for my husband and me as well. We are all blossoming because we are standing exactly in the right spot --- which brings me to an important truth: when we stand in precisely the destiny God has prepared for us, we will not only thrive but will make a difference for others in ways that can only happen through obedience to being in that place at that assigned time.

Think about your own life. Is there a time when you knew you were in the zone of God's destiny for you? Are you there now, or have you stepped away from His plans? I was a middle school teacher, and for years, that was my calling. I loved my job, and I cherished the children --- middle school students who often drove others crazy, and yet, I loved spending every single day with them. I taught with passion and believe I made a difference, but it was only because I was walking out God's calling for me. When we are obedient to His calling for our lives (as opposed to our human "good ideas"), He can use us and bless us in ways that are unimaginable!

Proverbs 16: 19 says this: "A man's heart plans his way, but the LORD determines his steps." (HCSB) And in Psalm 37:23, we find these words: "The LORD directs the steps of the godly. He delights in every detail of their lives." (New Living Translation) You see, God is willing, able, and ready to direct our steps if we will just let Him. He wants to place us in the destiny in which we will thrive and grow, also having an impact on others as we walk out His ordered plans for us. But to find ourselves in this place, we must give our wills over to His. We must pursue Him and His plans for us. We must allow ourselves to go to the "promised land" He has prepared for us, even if it looks scary at first.

My sweet husband, Dan, had a dream that we would live on this land, but I know for sure that he only had that vision because God laid it on his heart. Drawing those first plans and committing to living here were scary steps because we are both in retirement years, but the more we spent time here, the more we knew that this was where we were supposed to be. And there's more. As I walked and prayed, I promised God that this precious gift would be used for others, and we are holding true to that promise. God laid it on my heart to use this home for women's Bible study, and we are studying faithfully! We share our space with family, and we open our ponds to those who love to fish, even allowing a local church to host a kids' fishing tournament here. I am sharing my love of gardening with my granddaughters and teaching them the names of plants and the proper care of each one. One day, I plan to pass on this beautiful inheritance and I am preparing their hearts for that very day.

My plants are thriving because they are where they need to be, and this is a powerful lesson for all of us. We must surrender to God's plans and His steps for our lives, and when we do, He can give us blessings beyond measure and imagination. But surrender we must. Just this week, I have surrendered my will on some decisions that could have frightened me, but I am trusting God to do what He always does: take care of me when I delight in following His will.

I don't know where you are in your destiny today, and maybe, like me, you're in a new part of your life that requires new prayers for a new land. Trust God today and every day for everything He has in store for you . . . indeed, you have a wonderful inheritance!

LORD, YOU ALONE ARE MY INHERITANCE, MY CUP OF BLESSING.
    You guard all that is mine.
⁶ The land you have given me is a pleasant land.
    What a wonderful inheritance! (Psalm 16:5, NLT)

A Storm of Complaining

"When I complain about everyday things, I lack gratitude to God and express my failure to rely on His grace. . . Grumbling is no small thing, and I need to remember that God doesn't take it lightly." *Journey* devotional (*Journey: A Woman' Guide to Intimacy with God* from Lifeway)

When we need to hear a Word from God and we slow down to listen, He always comes through. Always. This morning when I awoke, I knew I needed to sit still, taking time to write in my journal; to read and pray. I failed to do that yesterday because I let life's inconveniences frustrate me and make me feel like I was drowning. I know better; I just didn't *do* better. Well, today I did what I know to do, and God came through with His faithfulness and His mercies, which are new every morning.

Yesterday was one of those days when life's inconveniences wore me out. I thought I wasn't complaining, but every time I went through the list of issues in my head, I was complaining . . . just quietly. Still, it's complaining. This morning's perfectly timed devotional reminded me that we are not to complain about anything. As Christians we are supposed to be a bright star in a "crooked" world, and I can't be that if I let complaining about life's issues get the best of me. I want to shine brightly, so I have asked God for His morning mercies today, and He is surely providing.

Just a few moments ago as I sat down to write this, I looked out my window and saw a pair of white cranes on my big pond. I have never seen them together before, and this sight reminded me of just how blessed we are by God's creation. My concern over my TV and dishwasher not working is so insignificant when I compare what they offer to what God offers. Just now, a red-winged blackbird, a regular visitor, landed on the feeder right in front of my window. Who needs TV? This beauty is the stuff that makes my heart leap!

If you need to find a new perspective today, be intentional about walking in gratitude, not complaining at all about whatever comes against you. Look around you and see all that God has done. Find beauty in His creation; find joy in the simple things of life; find peace in quiet moments and in the laughter of children. Don't let Satan drag you down the path of complaining . . . keep your focus on the One who made you and loves you completely.

Be blessed today and be grateful.

Early Morning Blue

I love to get up early in the morning, sit in my sunroom, and watch the view change as the sun comes up. Recently, I noticed something both beautiful and interesting that I had never noticed before: very early, before the sun is fully up, the panes of glass in my wall of windows look blue. Not a soft blue, but a deep rich hue. Blue has always been my favorite color, and this vision amazes and blesses me every time I see it. My intellectual brain knows that the panes of glass are clear; but for those few minutes, they take on the very richness of the morning sky, appearing to be blue themselves. It's incredible, and it reminds me of a spiritual principle.

Our daily walk with God should make us look as "blue" as Jesus. It should cause us to look more and more like Him, taking on His characteristics and color. Our blue should be so vibrant that we stand out in a dark world where sin strips the beautiful colors God intends for us to display. So in Godly terms, what should this look like?

First, Jesus loved. Period. He loved everyone. He loved His Father, His family, His disciples, and sinners. He even loved the Pharisees; He just didn't agree with them. Our daily walks must look like, feel like, and smell like love . . . for every single person we encounter. We must love the impatient ones, the mean ones, the rude ones, and the hurtful ones. We must love those with whom we disagree and love our enemies completely. It's a tall order, but Jesus commanded it. John 13: 34 documents this urgent command: "I give you a new command: Love one another. Just as I have loved you, you must also love one another." (HCSB) He loved his enemies and his friends, strangers and sinners, and we must do the same to take on the heart of Jesus, displaying His love to a hurting world.

Second, Jesus spent time alone with His Father. He secluded Himself, going into the wilderness and later into the Garden of Gethsemane to pray. We don't have to go into complete seclusion, but we must find places and times to be alone with God, our Father. Some people use a prayer closet, and others use a quiet office. I sit in my porch before my husband wakes up so I can read my Bible and/or study book and talk to God to start my day. Sometimes I walk outside on our land and seek God there. Wherever it works for you, you must do the same. It's great to pray with others, and I do that as well, but we have to spend time alone with God, seeking His face and emptying ourselves into His presence. And the more we spend time seeking Him first, the more we will be transformed to be like Him, to take on His loving, forgiving nature. Blue like Him.

Third, Jesus forgave . . . everybody. Even at the end of His earthly life as He hung on the Cross, He forgave those who scourged His body and pierced His hands, feet and sides. He extended forgiveness to sinners everywhere He went, and He expects us to do the same. Years ago, my older son, Asher, forgave a young woman who had hurt him, taking her back into his life. When I commented about how proud I was of his forgiving heart, he said, "Mom, I learned it from your example. You forgave my dad for everything wrong that happened in your marriage." He was watching, and I am so grateful that God enabled me to forgive. Let me be clear: *God* made a forgiving heart possible; He always enables us to do what we cannot do in our own human strength. Forgiveness is a command in scripture, and we find it in multiple places, but this reference, for me, is the one that brings it home: "For if you forgive men their trespasses, your Heavenly Father will also forgive you." (Matthew 6:14, HCSB). *If* we forgive . . . and so we must. A beautiful heart of true forgiveness, just like Jesus.

And finally, Jesus spent time with those who needed Him most: the sinners that others shunned. He talked with the woman at the well, knowing that she needed forgiveness and acceptance. He spent time with Zaccheus, a rich tax collector who was disliked and not trusted by others. He preached to the multitudes and accepted a former woman of ill repute into his following. Jesus didn't hold up in the temple and pray all day; He went to where hurting people walked and lived, healing their hearts and bodies and showing them the love of the Father. We must do likewise. Our churches must be outward focused and missional in spirit. We must get beyond the walls of our sanctuaries and meet a hurting world, not being afraid to get our hands dirty to take the love of Christ to those who need it most. Safe? Not always. But it is what Jesus commanded --- to go into the world and tell others about Him, just as He told them about the Father.

I pray that, like my windows, you will take on the colors around you . . . the colors of a Savior like no other. And the more you do, the more beautiful you will become!

Tethered

I teach a class, or two, at Horry-Georgetown Technical College and recently, I invited some of my students to my home for some down-time and fellowship. Some of the girls, feeling brave, decided to take one of our small boats onto the biggest pond. We could hear their giggles across the water, and every now and then we would hear a shriek of panic. There was a moment when they weren't sure they could get back to shore, and I thought to myself: "I should have tied a rope to the boat, just in case they got in trouble!" But I didn't, and they did eventually make it back to the dock, laughing at themselves all the way. It was such a fun and relaxing day with some incredible young people, but their boat experience left me thinking about needing to be tethered to a safe harbor.

Tether: to fasten or restrain by or as if by a tether (a rope or chain), meant to keep something (usually an animal) in a particular place.

I grew up watching westerns with my Dad, and I remember seeing the horses tethered to a post when the men had business in town. Tethered, so they wouldn't stray.

So what does this say about us? Well, this idea has me thinking about my own life, which just might help you to think about yours. Let me share a part of my story.

I was born Nancy Jean Bishop, raised in a Christian home and surrounded by a safe neighborhood filled with other Christian families. Even before I accepted Christ for my-self, God tethered me to Himself through my family and my church. His prevenient grace was wooing me even then to become the daughter He designed me to be. Did I stray in my teen years? Oh, yes, I did, but He kept drawing me back, tethered by His hand of grace.

At twenty-two years old, I became Jean Bishop Blocker, marrying a young man I loved, but marrying him without asking God for His guidance. We were young, and though we were both Christians, we were spiritually immature. I believed in myself more than God: "If I work hard enough, this marriage will make it." It didn't, but God was always there, drawing me into His redemptive arms. Tethered by His forgiveness.

In those eight years of my first marriage, I lost a pregnancy, lost my mother, gave birth to two beautiful children, and had some of the toughest years of my teaching career. I called out to God in crisis and I was almost 100% faithful in church attendance and serving God at my church, but I didn't have an active prayer and study life. Did God give up on me? Was He there through those devastating years? Yes, He was. He never deserted me, and looking back, I know that He honored my service and my dedication to raise my children to know Him. Tethered to Him by uncon-ditional love.

In 1989, I became Jean B. Burden, marrying for a second

time. If you look at statistics, we should have been one! Dan and I had both been in failed marriages, and we started our relationship with four children! But one huge difference came into play: before I ever met Dan, I had prayed this prayer: "God, give me a good man or let me live alone to raise my children." And Dan showed up --- an answer to prayer. His proposal of marriage was met with a few simple conditions, two of which were that we would never . . . **never** . . . consider divorce to be a possibility again and we would be involved in church --- deeply involved. With God's help, we have held to both of these since that very day, but this was only possible because we chose to recognize that God was there, tethering us to His possibilities and blessings.

This story could go on with many more examples, but here's what I know for sure. Even before we realize it, God is out there, drawing us into relationship with him; this is called His prevenient grace. And when we accept His offer, allowing Him to "be the boss" of our hearts and lives, He tethers us to Himself and we are never, ever without Him. Just like the prodigal son who ran away to the far country but eventually came home to his father's open arms, our Father stands with heart and arms open, waiting on us every day. He waits for us to call on His name, to seek Him above all else, and to love Him completely.

So back to the definition of our word: something is tethered to keep it in a particular place. God's great tether, even when we are ignoring Him and trying our best to stray, keeps us in a particular place: a place called grace. A place called unconditional love. A place called forgiveness. A place called blessing.

I encourage you to look at your life story. Think about the times when maybe, like me, you were not seeking God but He was always there, keeping you tethered to Him. He may have let you stray quite a bit because God does give us free will, but He was always there, waiting to pull us back to Him. Waiting to redeem us. Waiting with expectation, knowing that His love is the only thing that fills that mighty hole in our human hearts.

Hearts and minds tethered to God . . . what a beautiful connection!

Long Obedience in One Direction

As I was riding the lawnmower this morning, going on the fourth hour of mowing down and back, down and back, I couldn't help but think how some things in life just require a long turn of obedience. We moved to our new home in 2015, and this is our first summer of living on Boggy Road. The mowing is a huge task, requiring long mornings and afternoons of nothing but perseverance, but when it's done, it's a beautiful sight! I've been thinking about obedience lately in yoga class as well. When I started yoga over a year ago, ease in the moves seemed like a lifetime away, but today, I am moving more fluently, feeling less pain, and sure of my increased strength. It didn't happen overnight; in fact, it took quite a while just to get comfortable with the poses, and it required an even longer time to gain enough strength to do some of them with any semblance of grace and stability. (Some days were just ugly!)   There are plenty of other tasks in life that take long obedience in a single direction. Preparing to be an Olympic athlete . . . breaking an old, bad habit . . . eating a healthy diet. Long obedience in one direction, headed toward a goal. And then there's faith.

When I was younger, my prayers went something like this: I had a crisis; I prayed desperately. I needed something to happen? I prayed. But in between those "crisis" prayers, I wasn't so committed to my relationship with Christ. And studying God's Word wasn't even on my radar. After all, I was too busy. You know the story . . . busy being a working mom, busy raising a house filled with active children, busy being a wife, and even busy in church.

But I wasn't busy about the real business of God.

I was going through some impressive motions, and I really was doing some good things. But there comes a moment when you just know you have to create a new lifestyle of prayer and study. For me, that began to happen about 20 years ago.

I was rarely attending Sunday School at the time. Oh, I was there, however, I was "busy" getting ready for worship, practicing the organ or organizing music. I was too busy to sit in a classroom and learn. But God used the strangest thing to draw me to a Sunday School class, and I am so grateful that He did. After joining SS, I began attending a night Bible study at my church, and we read *The Purpose Drive Life* by Rick Warren. I love learning . . . always have, and when God transferred my love of learning to a hunger to know more about Him, He created a passionate woman who fell in love with the Word.

Then in 2006, another milestone moment occurred. I was seated at my first Joyce Meyer Conference in Winston-Salem. It was a Thursday evening, and I was so pitifully unprepared! I didn't have any paper on which to take notes, so when she said, "You need to write scriptures down in longhand," I was convicted! I hurried to the closest Barnes and Noble after the conference, bought my first journal, and the rest really is my spiritual history. I've been writing ever since, journaling scriptures, ideas from God, prayers, concerns, lessons from books I read . . . filling pages with small caveats, profound truths, and prayers to God.

And here's what I know for sure: studying God's Word and journaling have transformed me. It didn't happen overnight; it took long obedience in one direction, and that direction is God.

Since those early studies, I have read more Christian books than I can remember. I have taken notes on the powerful ones, and discussed a myriad of information with friends. I have completed Bible studies in small groups, doing the homework required to keep up! And I have absorbed books in the quietness of my own home, taking in ideas and knowledge that have changed my understanding. I have written key points from Sunday sermons and Wednesday night services, keeping all of this in my precious journals. But the most important habit has been going directly to God's word. And long obedience in that direction, coupled with prayers asking for wisdom and understanding, is transformative in ways that only God can orchestrate. Just as the Queen of Sheba went directly to Solomon (1 Kings) to learn from his wisdom, we must go directly to God. We must ask and listen, read and pray for enlightenment. We must invite the Holy Spirit to aid us as we seek to know more of God, our Father, and Jesus, our Savior. Long obedience in one direction, and that direction is God.

Do I sometimes slip? Oh, yes, I surely do. Some days I fail to study and pray, putting other things in front of God, but He always calls me back. Do I sometimes find it hard? Oh, yes! In yoga yesterday, I had the worst time ever! Everything seemed hard and my body fought me at every turn. But I didn't give up, and about 25 minutes into the class, things started to flow, and I'm so glad I stayed. It's the same with God. Sometimes it feels strangely hard, and maybe God seems distant, but just like in yoga, we have to push through and not quit, knowing that when we are faithful, God sees and blesses us every time.

Long obedience in one direction . . . right into the arms of God.

Let Your Heart Shine

I was in yoga class yesterday with a new instructor, Emily, and she said something a little different: "Let your heart shine." Now, I have heard other instructors say something similar like, "Lead with your heart," but this struck a chord in me. In yoga what she meant is this: in many poses the heart should be lifted toward the sky, and sometimes when we are standing with upper bodies bent over to the floor, we are to rise up, "leading with the heart." But she said a *different* thing: "Let your heart *shine*." That's when God started speaking into my hungry spirit in a hurry!

There are so many times in our lives when letting our hearts shine could make such a difference. We are living through difficult days in a hurting world. People need to see shining hearts and hear words of blessing and kindness, and yet, so many times, that's not happening. Children every day hear of their worthlessness; working adults are berated due to their mistakes but never praised for their accomplishments. Out-of-work men and women struggle with self-worth, feeling defeated by the hopelessness of their current situations. It's hard to let your heart shine when it is weighed down with stress, fear, and anxiety. So what can *we* do? How can *our* shining hearts help to change a world in crisis?

Just this morning I saw a video of a young man who started out selling ice cream to children for money. He pulled his cooler with a bicycle, and he noticed something in a hurry: many children didn't even have one dollar to purchase this sweet, cool treat. So what did he do? He got creative and let his heart shine in those neighborhoods. He found sponsors who would help him pay for the ice cream, and now he gives it away to children who cannot afford it, but he also asks for something in return. Each child who receives ice cream has to write a thank you note to one of the sponsors. Just that simple. He makes their days brighter and they learn the value of saying thank you. Is it working? Oh, yes, evidenced by his eight ice cream cycles driving all over the city! He decided to let his heart shine by sharing with children of poverty, and he is surely making a difference. But it can be even easier than this.

I ran into a young couple last week in a nail salon. It was the young woman's birthday, and they were discussing what they could afford: a manicure or a haircut, but not both. I remember those days when I had to make choices every single day... buy groceries or pay my car payment. Those were hard days. I remember them with thanksgiving because they changed me. Anyway, God nudged my spirit at that moment to give up my manicure and share with them. I reached into my wallet, handed her young man a $20 bill, and told them to have a good birthday. He argued with me, but I told him that God is very bossy and he best not argue with *Him!* He accepted and the young girl hugged me. Our hearts were shining together in that moment, and I left there with a joy in my spirit and a new plan for my day. I bought my own gel polish, treated myself at home, and enjoyed every minute of it! But letting your heart shine can be even easier than this.

Go to Wal-Mart and speak to every single person you see, sharing your smile and your kindness with your heart. It doesn't matter how they respond in turn; it only matters that *your* heart was shining. Go to McDonald's (or "*Old* McDonald's as my granddaughter, Harper, calls it) and pay for someone's meal in the drive-through. Go to the Post Office and offer to carry a heavy package for someone who is struggling. Like my friend Ann, whose church offers drive-through prayer, slow down and offer to pray for a stranger who appears sad or overwhelmed. I will never forget when a young employee of Chick-Fil-A in my town followed my 8 ½ months-pregnant daughter and me out the door. My daughter, Whitney, had been talking to me in line about her severe back pain, and the employee had obviously overheard us. She decided to let her heart shine at that moment, asking my daughter if she could pray for her. We were humbled and grateful, and her shining heart affected ours.

Other simple ideas? Ask your cashier at the grocery store how he/she is doing. Thank the worker for the job well-done. Notice people . . . and I mean, **REALLY** notice them. Tell the girl behind the counter what a beautiful smile she has. These simple things can change the course of someone's day. Simple kindness shared through letting your heart shine. And isn't that what God has asks of us?

He first asks us to love *Him*. Above all else, it's about *Him*. Then He commands us to love others. And I like to think that He expects us to love people aggressively, quietly, sweetly, and passionately. We are to love them with our shining hearts, through our words, our actions, and our attitudes. And just like the domino effect, I believe our small acts of shining hearts can tumble over into love being spread everywhere we go. And I don't know about you, but I seem to go a lot of places with plenty of opportunities to shine!

So today and every day: be intentional. Follow Jesus' command to love by letting your heart shine so others can clearly see Him through you. They just might want to know the source of your joy, and then you can tell them!

Love the LORD your God with all your heart, with all your soul, and with all your strength. (Deuteronomy 6:5, HCSB)

"One of the scribes approached [Jesus]. When he heard them debating and saw that Jesus answered them well, he asked Him, "Which command is the most important of all?" [29] "This is the most important," Jesus answered: Listen, Israel! The Lord our God, the Lord is One. [30] Love the Lord your God with all your heart, with all your soul, with all your mind ,and with all your strength. [31] "The second is: Love your neighbor as yourself. There is no other command greater than these." (Mark 12:28-31, HCSB)

"For the entire law is fulfilled in one statement: Love your neighbor as yourself." (Galatians 5:14, HCSB)

**This devotional is dedicated to my friend and instructor, Emily. Thank you for always letting your heart shine for others!

An Unexpected Brownie

Sometimes in life we receive an unexpected blessing, a "never-saw-this-coming" kind of blessing. This summer our surprise blessing is named Brownie. He began hanging around our new home back in May, and I knew even then that something was up (other than my two female labs!). I really thought we lived too far out to attract company. I truly did have a false sense of security about the whole business of heat and dogs, but Brownie, in his persistence, managed to find my girls anyway. Here's the odd thing: he never left. I am writing this at the very end of July, and he's still here. So I guess I need to tell you about our new boy.

Brownie should probably be named Golden, but my granddaughters, Lily and Harper, decided he would be called Brownie and that was the end of that. He is a beautiful golden color, probably a Golden Retriever, and his middle name should be Cautious. As spring has progressed to summer, he has moved closer and closer to our house, resting in the shade and drinking from our water bowls. Of course, I starting feeding him because I would never let a child or an animal go hungry, so he became part of my daily routine. Each week, I move his bowls closer to the house, and he moves with them. Just before I came inside this evening, he was lying under a pine tree, eyeing me. There's only one problem: he only "eyes" us. He won't let us near him, and if we make eye contact, he moves back. My son-in-law tried to coax him closer; when Chris sat down, Brownie sat down, and when Chris got up, so did the dog. When we cut grass, he runs near us, but only if we're not looking. I really want him to be my forever dog, and I hope my food and treats will eventually win him over, but in the meantime, he has reminded me of some truth.

God is out there, waiting for us to make eye contact . . . waiting for us to move closer to Him. He isn't waiting with duck jerky treats and water, but He's waiting nonetheless. He waits with open arms, compassion, boundless grace, and Fatherly love. He waits with patience, wooing us closer and closer into His presence. And when we hang back, refusing to connect with Him, He waits anyway, never giving up on us being His forever children.

Some of us have committed to being His, and yet, some days, we avoid eye contact. We harbor guilt or unforgiveness for others and even ourselves, and if we truly look into His eyes, we just might have to admit our weakness. We start the day, bounding into our to-do lists, and we fail to look in His eyes and seek His face. And the more we avoid eye-contact, the more we just might develop a fear that somehow, He doesn't love us anymore. Well, let's get this straight: He adores us. No matter what. No matter how much attention you have given Him lately. No matter what you've done or not done. **He adores You.** With the beauty of His morning sky and colors of summer, He is constantly wooing you to come closer and spend time in His presence. And no matter how many times you back away, He won't give up on you. What an incredible picture of love!

And there's one more thing: every day I make it a point to give my dogs lots of love in front of Brownie. I rub their heads, scratch their necks, kiss their sweet faces, and speak blessings over them.

You see, I want Brownie to want what I have to offer: tenderness, a home of protection, and unconditional love, and I hope if he sees it enough, he will eventually join us in this sweet circle of love. God is loving on people all around you. He is blessing them and pouring out His heart, drawing them into His circle called Redemption. Look around. See the goodness of God, and let it create a hunger in your heart for what He can give. Just like I want to give Brownie a forever home, God wants the same for all of us . . . **every single person** in the world. He wants to give everyone the safe "cleft in the rock" and the awesomeness of being loved by the Creator of this entire universe. Can it get any better than this?

And what about those of us who have already stepped toward Him and continue to live in His presence every day? What is *our* responsibility to those who haven't made eye contact with Him? Our blessed and joyous task is to live every single day, letting others see the joy of living as His children, to let them see that life with God and with our Savior is *so good* that they will want what we have. And just like I pray that Brownie will eventually accept my invitation to be a part of our Boggy Road family, I pray that others will hunger to be a part of the heavenly chorus, both now and forevermore. Amen.

Shhh . . . Be Quiet!

I've had my daughter's dog, Cindy, for the past couple of weeks, and Cindy has "had" me. She greets me as soon as my feet hit the floor at 5:00 A.M, and she trembles with anticipation until I pour my first cup of coffee and head to the door. When I pick up her leash, she is beside herself with excitement, and once the door is open, she literally drags me into the yard . . . all 20 pounds of her. At this time of year when the early morning weather is perfect and the night sky is incredibly stunning, I love our morning walk, and I am grateful to Cindy for making me go outside instead of sit in my "study" chair. And yes, there is a point to this mundane story. . .

As Cindy and I have walked in these past weeks, I have been repeatedly awed by the wonder of the night sky. These walks have become more than Cindy's morning constitutional; they have become my time with God. I have greeted Him, talked with Him, and praised Him for everything imaginable . . . for the beauty of nature, for the constellations (I can only pick out three . . . remedial astronomy is needed), for answered prayers, and for His love. But this morning, the walk took on new life: it became worship. I have had worship on my mind a lot lately because I think too many people in the church have lost their sense of worship, and it is the very thing for which we are created! We come to church thinking someone is supposed to "feed" us or that we will be entertained, but this is farthest from the right motive; we should enter God's house and God's world to worship Him. And this morning as I gazed at the sky, I worshiped God in beauty and holiness. It was quite a moment. But there's more.

Last night, two of my daughters and my precious granddaughter, Olivia, came home for dinner with the family. Olivia is three months old, and she is just starting to "talk." Now, we know *not* to talk baby talk to Olivia because we want her to learn language . . . after all, language is what I do as a teacher! But Meredith said something interesting: she read somewhere that we should ask Olivia questions and then wait on her to answer. Interesting process for a three-month old, but I've been doing it, and guess what . . . when I talk and then hush, she talks back! It's amazing! Of course, I'm sure it's because she's a genius (I'm being playful but I'm not exaggerating). When we spoke to her and asked questions and then closed our mouths long enough for her to respond, she did . . . every single time! And again, this led me to God.

How many times do we go to God in prayer and then *WE* do all the talking? How many times do we ask Him for things and then never hush just to listen for His still, small voice? How many times do we miss His incredible nudging in our day because we never get still and quiet enough to feel Him and know His presence? This morning, I got that message loud and clear. I walked, and talked, and then? I just walked and listened. What an awesome way to start the day!

I pray that in the coming days, you will remember God's call to be still and quiet in His presence. Make it a priority every single day, especially early in the morning. Days are always better when we give God the first fruits of our time, talking to Him and then listening for the words He wants to speak over our lives. There's a prayer I learned during an Emmaus weekend and it begins like this: "Come, Holy Spirit; fill the hearts of Your faithful and kindle in us the fire of Your love." Pray that the Holy Spirit will fill your heart and your listening ears as you walk your daily journey with God!

1 Kings 19: 11-12, "Then He said, "Go out and stand on the mountain in the LORD's presence. At that moment, the LORD passed by. A great and mighty wind was tearing at the mountains and was shattering cliffs before the LORD, but the LORD was not in the wind. After the wind there was an earthquake, but the LORD was not in the earthquake. [12] After the earthquake there was a fire, but the LORD was not in the fire. And after the fire there was a voice, a soft whisper." (HCSB)

"He says, "Be still, and know that I am God;
I will be exalted among the nations,
I will be exalted in the earth." (Psalm 46:10, NIV)

NOTE: This was written in September 2010, but I just re-discovered it while writing this book! God knew I needed to hear it again, so maybe you did, too! ☺

Choose To Let it Go!

Recently a family member leaked information about a purchase my "farmer" husband had made without telling me. I was more than a little surprised, and quite honestly, I was irritated . . . not because he didn't tell me, but because he told someone else without including me. This is not at all like him, but it was a very big purchase. He agreed with his friend, the seller, to make payments over time, and so he was waiting to tell me until payments were complete. Oops. The secret got out, and needless to say, we had a heart to heart. I was quick to say that I really couldn't argue about the purchase since he makes the money to pay for it. Still, the secretiveness bothered me.

In the next few days, I thought a lot about what he did, I gave him a light-hearted hard time, and I pondered it some more. Then God reminded me of something so very important: I needed to forgive and forget about it, by not choosing to battle on and on. It's not the easiest thing to do.

Then something happened to me at work --- something that wasn't fair, wasn't right, and wasn't expected. Someone else made an error that affected me, and it couldn't be corrected. I made all the right phone calls, explained the situation politely and professionally, but all I got was an apology. No rectifying the problem. Just an apology. My sweet husband let me vent for a few minutes, and then he said, "Sometimes you just have to let things go, especially when there is absolutely nothing you can do to change it." Sage advice from the man who secretly spent $4,000 on a tractor implement! ☺

But, he's right. Sometimes in life, things aren't fair. People hurt our feelings by their actions, and we have to make a choice. People make mistakes that cost us something, and we have to make a choice. People do things that disappoint us terribly, and we have to make a choice. The choice? To let go, forgive, and move on. One caveat, again from my smart man: sometimes things that happen to us are huge, and other times they are just trivial but aggravating. We do have to see the difference and prayerfully consider how God would have us handle each situation.

When I look back over my life, God has "moved on" more times than I can count. I have approached Him, begging forgiveness, and He has set the perfect model by forgiving and moving on. He doesn't continue to hold my actions against me. Scripture promises us this in Psalm 103: 12: "As far as the east is from the west, so far has He removed our transgressions from us." (HCSB) Why in the world does He do that when He could hold it against me forever? He does it because He loves me, and He loves you, too. And just as this is our history with Him today, we see this same history in the Bible over and over. The Israelites repeatedly turned their hearts away from Him, even after He had been so very good to them, and yet, He continued to forgive and give them ways to move forward. What an incredible picture of our heavenly Father!

So back to us. Our fleshly, sin nature tells us to rant and rave

when we are mistreated. It tells us to demand that things be rec-
tified! But sometimes, God is just asking us to humble ourselves
before Him, trust Him in every situation, and let it go! It doesn't
matter what someone did to us or how much we are hurt, offend-
ed, or angered. God is bigger, wiser, and more powerful than all
of this, and when we give our hearts completely to Him, He truly
can help us let go of everything . . . even the things we believe to
be impossible to release.

This morning God has reminded me to trust Him. And in the coming days, I'm sure He will have to remind me --- and you --- again.
But He will. You see, even when we are not faithful, He remains
faithful to us, His children and heirs of His kingdom.

"Great is Thy faithfulness! Great is Thy faithfulness! Morning by
morning new mercies I see. All I have needed Thy hand hath
provided. Great is Thy faithfulness, Lord unto me!" (Thomas
Chisholm)

My prayer for all of us is that we allow God's daily mercies to help
us answer to Him and not to the frustrations and vexations of this
world. We really can let it go!

"Because of the LORD'S GREAT LOVE WE ARE NOT CONSUMED,
      for his compassions never fail.
23 They are new every morning;
      great is your faithfulness.
24 I say to myself, "The LORD IS MY PORTION;
      therefore I will wait for him."   (Lamentations 3: 22-24)

Unintentional

I am responsible for the death of my first baby. I didn't mean to do it, and I surely didn't plan it. There was no malice; in fact, I wanted that baby more than anything else in the world. But still, I was the cause of the end of an otherwise healthy pregnancy, and at the end of the day on August 5, 1981, my baby was gone.

The morning started out beautifully. I packed my car, gave my husband a ride to work at a new job, and headed to our church. We were taking the children on a field trip, and I was so excited. As I left my husband's workplace, I did what drivers do every day: I allowed myself to be distracted. My first husband and I fought on the way to work . . . not an unusual thing for us. As I drove away, I turned my mind to other things --- things like finding something in my purse, and that was the last thing I remember for days. You see, in my distraction with useless things like lipstick, I ran a stop sign, and it was a careless mistake that changed me forever. Many hours later, I was taken into surgery to remove a ruptured spleen, but the long day's wait proved to be too long for my sweet little one. Five days later, I delivered a 20-week, dead fetus.

Okay, I know this is a little morose, but there's a point. I allowed carelessness to cost me the very thing I hungered for most in the world: to be a mother. I allowed distraction to almost cost me my own life. I didn't start school on time that fall because my body and mind both needed time to rest and heal. I cried and I grieved, but the end result was still an empty womb and a broken heart. And it was my fault.

Sometimes in life, we are thrown into horrible situations that we didn't cause. Someone we love faces cancer, or we lose a job and find ourselves destitute. Sometimes we jump feet first into bad situations because we haven't learned how to change our own habits. And then, sometimes, we fall into despair because we are careless, ridiculously careless.

A young person dies in an accident because she was on a cell phone.
A beautiful young woman falls into drug addiction because she trusts a young man and stops thinking for herself.

A husband or wife feels lonely and hopeless and finds someone who understands . . . and it turns into an affair.

We never meant for these things to happen. We didn't plan them. But they happened anyway, and these life-altering events can destroy us, but they don't have to. With God, there is always hope. In the Old Testament we find these words of hope:

"The LORD your God is with you,
    the Mighty Warrior who saves.
He will take great delight in you;
    in his love he will no longer rebuke you,
    but will rejoice over you with singing."   (Zephaniah 3:17)

Our God is a mighty Warrior who saves, and He promises to be with us. Nowhere in scripture does it say that He only is with us when things happen to us that we didn't cause. Nowhere does it say that He gives up on us when we are foolish and careless. It says that He is with us. He saves us. He loves us.

In the days after my miscarriage, I struggled. *Really* struggled. A few days after I got home from the hospital, I was resting in my recliner, and God sent me an angel in the form of Phil Donahue. Yes, Phil Donahue. If you're not as old as I am, you might not know who he is, but he was the talk-show king before Oprah and Ellen. God sent him directly into my living room on a very sad day in August. I had the remote in hand, and as I turned the channels, looking for something to drive away the boredom and the pain, I found Phil Donahue. Guess what he was talking about with his panel . . . recovering from miscarriage. I don't remember everything they said that day, but I do remember this: they said that it's okay to grieve and it's okay for others not to understand my pain. People don't mean to be hurtful when they say things like, "You'll have another one." They just don't understand. I needed comfort. I needed emotional permission to be incredibly sad, and I found it with Phil Donahue. I'm very sure that the God who loves me . . . and loves you, too . . . sent me to that channel on that very day. You see, God can use anything to help us heal, even when we've been careless.

There's another thing: scripture tells us that God holds our tears.

Psalm 56:8, says it this way:

> You've kept track of my every toss and turn
>   through the sleepless nights,
> Each tear entered in your ledger,
>   each ache written in your book. (*The Message*)

God wouldn't write my tears in His ledger if He didn't love me. He wouldn't keep track of my sleepless nights, hurting over the loss of my child, if He didn't adore me.

Time doesn't heal all wounds; God does.

Sometimes pain is so deep and pervasive that we just don't think we can find our way out. I remember going to my mother's house, falling into her arms as soon as she opened the front door, and crying because I could not speak. She understood, holding me until my sobs subsided, and she didn't try to make light of my heartache. She didn't say, "You'll have another one." She just loved me in the way that God loved her. She passed on His unconditional love while I lay in her arms.

My pastor helped me, too. His name was Posey Belcher, and he was one amazing man of God. He walked into my home, and instead of saying, "How are you?", he said, "How are you . . . *really*?" Two very different questions. I was so glad that someone wanted to know how horrible I really felt, and his listening ears were another reminder of God's healing love. He listened, he prayed for me, and he nodded in understanding. And when he left, I knew that God had sent him to me.

Just like God sent Phil Donahue, God gave me my mother and my pastor at a time that I simply couldn't get through the pain without comfort from a friend with "skin on."

Maybe as you read this, you are struggling to recover from a terrible loss . . . maybe one that you caused yourself. Maybe you know a friend who can barely keep moving due to grief and you don't know what to do. Hear these words: God loves us, feels our pain, and will hold onto us until we can stand again. If our friend is in pain, He can use us to do what others did for me: be the body of Christ to those in need by simply loving, holding, and listening --- not trying to provide human answers but just by being present.

Wherever you find yourself, know this: my prayer for you comes from Romans 15:13 --- "May the God of hope fill you with all joy and peace as you trust in him, so that you may overflow with hope by the power of the Holy Spirit." (NIV)

I also pray that you will, in the words of Psalm 23, "rest beside still waters" so your soul may be restored and healed.

Careless or not, God has adopted you as His child, and He is waiting to heal your heart. Let Him in today, allowing Him to do His best work in you, that you may glorify Him all the days of your life.

Prayer for 2017 or Any New Year with God

Father, it is hard to believe that we are here again, at the beginning of a new year. Let us all be thankful for another day, another year, and another chance to make a difference in Your name.

Father, forgive us for wasted money, wasted time, and wasted energy. Show us how to use Your resources in a way that honors the gifts, for every single thing we have is a gift from You.

Father, forgive us for thinking it's all about us. This world is so self-centered, and even when we serve You in our churches and our communities, it is easy to lose sight of You, making it all about us, our convenience, and our wants. Please help us to remember Your great sacrifice for us, and let us always give back and give out with a heart of gratitude and humility.

Father, forgive those of us who claim you as ours for not behaving in a way that makes it obvious to whom we belong. Help us to see ourselves the way You see us, and convict our hearts to test every word and every action against *Your* Word.

Father, break our hearts for what breaks Yours. Open our eyes to see the work You are already doing around us, and order our steps to serve You in the places You have ordained for us. Please don't let us start something and expect You to bless it; let us always start with You, and ask You to show us what You would have us do.

Father, thank you for the warm days we have experienced in December of this year. People everywhere . . .the homeless and those without adequate heat . . . have surely breathed a sigh of relief. Let us not complain about wanting a white Christmas and instead think of how others have been blessed.

Father, guide us as we pray diligently for our country. Let us never forget that we are a nation founded on Christian principles. Let us pray about what we can do to stand for You, and let us use our vote and our prayers to turn things around in this great nation.

Father, give us all the courage to open every space of our hearts to you. Let us hold nothing back, knowing and trusting that anything You ordain for us will be good. Let us trust You in the difficult moments and the celebrations of joy, having faith that You will use everything for Your good in some way.

Father, thank You for another year. Let us look ahead with anticipation and joy, but not so much that we cannot enjoy today . . . every moment You have given us. Let us start our year with hearts of gratitude and praise, and let us be known as Yours.

Father, help us to commit and stick with the most important resolution of all: to pray without ceasing and entrust all things to You. What we could do if only we would pray . . . I believe you would heal our land, our families, and our hearts!

With love and humility,

Your Servant

Works Cited

Fry, Steve. "Let It Be Said of Us." Maranatha! Music, 1994.

http://wwwyogajournal.com/article/beginners/the-meaning-of-quot-namaste-quot/

Gibson, Mel, Director and Producer. *Braveheart.* 1995.

Ortega, Domingo. Excerpt from "Bullfight Critics Ranked in Rows."

Shirer, Priscilla Shirer. *Armor of God*. Nashville: Lifeway Press, 2015.

Shirer, Priscilla. *Breathe.* Nashville, Lifeway Press, 2014.

Shirer, Priscilla. *Fervent*. Nashville: B&H Publishing Group, 2015.

Zaillian, Steven. Screenplay, *Schindler's List.* 1993.

Thank you for reading this devotional and for your continued support of Jean Burden's ministry. You may also wish to purchase Jean's first book from her ministry or from any online bookstore:

Reflections From the Parlor

A Pilgrim's Spiritual Journey

40 devotional writings to go along with personal prayer meditation and study

ISBN: 978-0-9910989-4-1

CPSIA information can be obtained
at www.ICGtesting.com
Printed in the USA
FFOW05n1052150517
35650FF

9 780991 098996